Mrs. C's Economics with Ease

A Workbook for *Microeconomics*

Marilyn Cottrell
Brock University

KENDALL/HUNT   PUBLISHING   COMPANY
4050 Westmark Drive   Dubuque, Iowa 52002

Dedication

To my wonderful husband, Alan, and my five beautiful children, Warren, Ian, Stuart, Rylan, and Ashleigh, five of whom chose to take at least one economics course to better understand my great love of economics. To Ian and Ashleigh, who chose economics as their major without regret. To my son Warren, who has always given me a special strength, understanding, and dedication in all that I do. Lost, but never forgotten. For your love and support, I will be eternally grateful.

Love grows as a family expands. To the joyous additions and love of my ever-growing family: Nicole, Ian's wife; Melissa, Stuart's wife; Michal, Rylan's wife; and Adam, Ashleigh's fiancé. Thank you for the happiness you bring to dad and to me.

CONTENTS

*Note: This text follows the chapters in ***Microeconomics***, Sixth Canadian Edition, by Michael Parkin and Robin Bade.

Acknowledgments

I would like to thank my colleagues, Professors Robert Dimand, Roberta Robb, and Lewis Soroka of Brock University for their invaluable assistance and guidance in not only this, but in many other scholarly endeavours. Special thanks are given to Indra Hardeen, Jennifer Baker and Chantel Mundell for reviewing the manuscript, and Karen Phillips, our administrative assistant.

I am truly grateful to have two wonderful young men who are always there for me: Robert Gemmell produces the most sensational graphics while Peter Gomes works my Macromedia Flash into an art form. Thank you for your patience, smiles, good humour and support.

To Microeconomics Students

Success in economics need not be elusive. Understanding the basic concepts of economics and the ability to do very straightforward problems will lead you, the student, to success in economics. Once you have mastered the basic problems, any questions that might be presented to you on a quiz, a test, or an exam will be seen as a variation of these problems or a change of the numbers within the problems.

Your confidence in the material will grow over time, and your ability to write tests will improve vastly. A little effort is involved in answering the questions for each chapter, but once done, you will see similar phrases in other questions, similar mathematical components needed, and you will be able to find the required answers to the questions that are posed to you.

It is imperative that you attempt each question prior to looking at the answers. There is a vast difference between seeing how a question is done and actually doing a question. When you look at an answer, the wording, the graph, or the mathematics, you can follow along, and it will make sense; however, reproducing a similar answer on an exam is vastly different. Can you remember the labelling of the graph? Which curves should appear on which graph? What causes the shifts of those curves? In which direction those shifts should move? If price changes, do you shift the curve or merely move along the curve? Only when you do these questions and do them prior to looking at the answers will you be able to first understand where in a particular problem you are having difficulties and where in a given chapter you are struggling.

Trying a problem, drawing a graph, and attempting the mathematics are all part of the process of learning. You do learn and retain that knowledge if you work a problem through and draw the graphs. There is something to be said for the old adage, 'Practice makes perfect'. One of the best ways to study for an economics test is to redo the problems and draw the graphs.

Much of the work that we do in economics is cumulative. To be able to understand this week's material, you have to make an effort to learn last week's material. The easiest way to do this is to adopt a weekly work plan.

As my good friend, Professor Soroka would always tell his classes:
> *Go to lectures. It is easier to learn when you hear explanations, write notes, and construct diagrams step-by-step. Each week, do the assigned problems, as well as some multiple-choice questions. Answering the problems and multiple-choice questions helps you to learn, and to find out if you understand the course material. Attend tutorials. Solve problems, review difficult material, and ask questions about anything you do not understand. Above all, do not get discouraged.*

This workbook is not meant to supplant either the text or study guide, but rather to be used in conjunction with them to assist you in understanding the material and increasing your chances of success. I hope you find economics as much fun as I do. Enjoy learning!

Marilyn Cottrell

PART ONE
AN INTRODUCTION TO MICROECONOMICS

Tutorial #1
Chapter 2: *The Economics Problem*

Assignment #1: Production Possibilities and Opportunity Cost

It is imperative that you make an effort to attempt all the questions assigned prior to your tutorial.

Multiple-Choice Questions:
Choose the one alternative that best completes the statement or answers the question.
Please note that many of the multiple-choice questions have been written in both question format and sentence-completion format to better assist you in understanding the wording of multiple-choice questions.
1. The Aviator Lake Music Company makes compact disc players and compact discs. The following table summarizes its production capacity.

Point	Production of Players (number/day)	Production of Discs (number/day)
a	0	400
b	4	360
c	8	280
d	12	160
e	16	0

Points on Aviator Lake Music Company's PPF

Use this information to answer the following question.
  Aviator Lake Music Company produces 8 players and 280 discs per day and will be increasing its daily player production to 12. The table shows that each additional player will cost:
a) 160 discs.
b) 120 discs.
c) 30 discs.
d) 13.3 discs.

2. A situation in which all resources in Aviator Lake Music Company are *not* fully utilized is represented in a production possibility frontier diagram by
a) any point on either the horizontal or vertical axis.
b) a point above or to the right of the production possibility frontier.
c) a point outside the production possibility frontier.
d) a point inside the production possibility frontier.

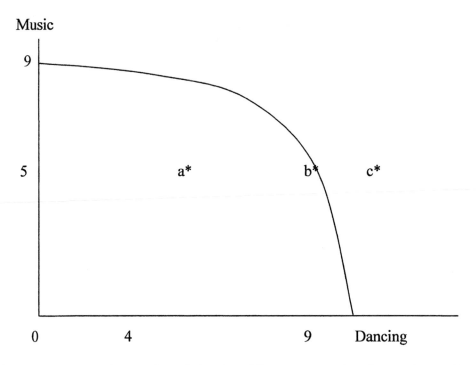

There are two goods: music and dancing. The next two questions refer to this diagram.

3. Refer to the preceding production possibility frontier. Which of the following is true about point a?
a) It is unattainable.
b) Although no more music can be produced, more dancing can be produced.
c) Resources are not fully employed.
d) It is preferred to point b.

4. In the preceding diagram,
a) movement from point a to point b would require a technological improvement.
b) point b is superior to point a.
c) some resources must be unemployed at point c.
d) the concept of decreasing opportunity cost is illustrated.

Short-Answer Questions:
1. There is an expression: 'You can't have your cake and eat it too'. Explain carefully which economic concept is illustrated in this statement and what it means.

2. Are the following questions positive or normative statements? Explain.
   (i) Aviator Stu, the Governor of the Central Bank of Aviator Lake, sets the interest rate at 4%.
   (ii) Aviator Ashleigh thinks the Central Bank of Aviator Lake should set the interest rate at 3.5%.

Problems:

1. Fog has rolled in on Aviator Lake, and all planes are grounded. Aviator Ashleigh is planning how to spend this foggy Sunday, and the choice is between watching DVDs on her computer (each lasting 2 hours) or studying her microeconomics textbook. She has 10 hours available to her. If she decides to study, she could read the following number of pages:

2 hours	80 pages
4 hours	130 pages
6 hours	160 pages
8 hours	175 pages
10 hours	180 pages

    a) Given this information, draw Aviator Ashleigh's production possibility curve between DVDs watched and pages of microeconomics studied.
    b) What happens to the opportunity cost of watching DVDs as more DVDs are watched? (Support your answer with calculations.)
    c) Could Aviator Ashleigh watch 3 DVDs and study 150 pages of her textbook? Explain.
    d) If Aviator Ashleigh has already read 160 pages, what is the opportunity cost of reading 1 more page? What is the opportunity cost of reading 15 more pages?
    e) If Aviator Ashleigh takes a speed-reading course, show the effect on her production possibility curve.

PART TWO
HOW MARKETS WORK

Tutorial #2
Chapter 3: *Demand and Supply*

Assignment #2: Demand and Supply Determinants, Schedules, Graphs, and Equations

Multiple-Choice Questions:
Choose the one alternative that best completes the statement or answers the question.
1. If the price of oil in Aviator Lake, a close substitute for Alberta's coal, increases, then
a) the supply curve for Alberta coal will shift to the right.
b) the demand curve for Alberta coal will shift to the right.
c) the equilibrium price and quantity of Alberta coal will not change.
d) the quantity of Alberta coal demanded will decline.

Short-Answer Questions:
1. If we observe a decrease in the price of computers in Aviator Lake and an increase in quantity traded, then we know that the supply of computers has increased. True/false? Explain.

2. What effect will the following have on the demand, supply, price, and quantity traded of Aviator Rylan's Fine Wines in Aviator Lake?
a) The number of wineries increases.
b) The price of beer increases.
c) A bad harvest occurs in the grape industry.
d) High winds and hailstorms rage through Aviator Lake. At the same time, more people are purchasing greater quantities of Aviator Rylan's Fine Wines.

3. Correct the following statements, if needed, so that there is correct usage of the terms "demand", "quantity demanded", "supply" and "quantity supplied".
a) As the price of Aviator Rylan's Fine Wine increases, consumers demand less Aviator Rylan's Fine Wine.
b) An increase in incomes of scooter buyers will increase the quantity demanded for scooters in Aviator Lake.
c) A decrease in the supply of fish means suppliers will provide fewer fish—whatever the current price is.
d) The price of bicycles-built-for-two in Aviator Lake increases if the supply of bicycles-built-for-two in Aviator Lake decreases.

4. An increase in the price of Aviator Lake Honey raises the price of sugar and increases the quantity of sugar traded. Therefore, sugar and Aviator Lake Honey are substitutes. True/false? Explain.

5. Technological innovations in the production of computers in Aviator Lake make the firms more productive. True/false?
Explain.

Problems:
1. Suppose that the supply and demand for Nikki's Aviator Lake Strawberries in the Nunavut market are as follows (the quantities are in thousands of kilos per week):

Price	Quantity Demanded	Quantity Supplied
$4.00	140	60
4.25	130	70
4.50	120	80
4.75	110	90
5.00	100	100
5.25	90	110
5.50	80	120

a) What are the equilibrium price and quantity of Nikki's Aviator Lake Strawberries in Nunavut?

b) The demand and supply equations for the preceding data are as follows
   Demand: $Q_D = 300 - 40P$ Inverse Demand curve: $[P = 7.5 - 0.025\ Q_D]$
   Supply: $Q_S = -100 + 40P$ Inverse Supply curve: $[P = 2.5 + 0.025\ Q_S]$
   Solve the equations for equilibrium price and quantity as a check on your answer in (a).

c) Use the equations to find the intercepts of the demand and supply curves for Nikki's Aviator Lake Strawberries. Plot the supply and demand curves for Nikki's Aviator Lake Strawberries showing the intercepts and the equilibrium price and quantity.

d) Suppose there is an increase in demand for Nikki's Aviator Lake Strawberries such that the equation for demand is now:
   $Q_D' = 380 - 40P$
   What is the new equilibrium price and quantity traded?

2. Suppose that Aviator Adam's Flying School students' demand for Aerodrome concert tickets is as follows:

Price	Quantity Demanded	Quantity Supplied
$ 6.00	8,000	
8.00	5,000	
9.00	2,500	
10.00	1,500	
11.00	1,000	

Concert pricing policy is set by Aviator Adam, who has decided that all seats will sell at the same price regardless of location or popularity of the performer (clearly,

5

Aviator Adam is a mechanical engineer and not an economist). Also, the only concert hall available is Aerodrome, and it has a seating capacity of 5,000.

a) If Aviator Adam sets a price of $10 per seat, is there an excess demand or supply of concert tickets in Aviator Lake?

b) What price would fill the Aerodrome concert hall without creating a shortage of seats?

c) Suppose the previous demand schedule refers to an "average" concert, and when a particularly popular performer is booked, the quantity of tickets demanded at each price doubles. What would be the equilibrium ticket price for a popular performer at Aerodrome?

d) Do you think ticket scalping would be more profitable if the price were set equal to, above, or below equilibrium? Explain.

Tutorial #3
Chapter 4: *Elasticity*

Assignment #3: Elasticity, Determinants, and Equations

Multiple-Choice Questions:
Choose the one alternative that best completes the statement or answers the question.
The following questions may be posed in the form of a multiple-choice question or they could be posed as a short-answer question. Seeing these small problems worked through will give you a better idea of how to answer, regardless of the question format.

1. If the price elasticity of demand for Aviator Lake Beer is 2 and price increases by 2%, the quantity demanded
a) decreases by 4%.
b) decreases by 1%.
c) decreases by 2%.
d) cannot be determined with this information.

2. Michal allocates $200 for her monthly expenditure on compact discs and decides to spend no more and no less, regardless of price. Michal's demand for compact discs is
a) perfectly inelastic.
b) perfectly elastic.
c) of unit elasticity.
d) less than one but greater than zero.

3. Which of the following is more likely to have an elastic demand?
a) Sea salt
b) Rye bread
c) Beef steak
d) 1% milk

4. Which of the following pairs of commodities is likely to have a cross-price elasticity of demand that is positive?
a) Hockey sticks and pucks
b) Rye bread and cheddar cheese
c) Tapes and compact discs
d) French perfume and garden hose

5. If the price elasticity of supply of blueberries in Aviator Lake is 0.1, this means that a
a) 0.1% increase in price is matched by a 0.1% increase in quantity supplied.
b) 10% decrease in price is associated with a 1% decrease in quantity supplied.
c) 10% increase in price will increase total revenue by 0.1%.
d) 1% decrease in price induces a 10% decrease in quantity supplied.

6. To avoid an increase in the local property tax, Aviator Ashleigh, who is the owner of Aviator Lake Cottages, proposes a 2% lodging tax. It is assumed that this tax would be shifted to tourists. The hotel/cottage rental industry owners argue that the tax would hurt business because tourists would go elsewhere. What the hotel/cabin owners were really saying is that
a) tourist demand is inelastic, so the tax would be passed onto the tourists.
b) tourist demand is very elastic, so hotels and cabins would have to bear the tax.
c) they would prefer a property-tax increase.
d) it is unfair to tax people who do not live in the area.

7. A necessity is
a) a normal good with an income elasticity that is less than one.
b) an inferior good.
c) a normal good with an income elasticity that is greater than one.
d) a normal good with an income elasticity of less than zero.

Short-Answer Questions:
1. In each of the following scenarios in Aviator Lake, indicate whether the event deals with own-price elasticity, cross-price elasticity, or income elasticity. If own-price elasticity, indicate whether demand is elastic, inelastic, or unit elastic; if cross-price elasticity, indicate whether the goods are complements or substitutes; if income elasticity, indicate whether the good is inferior or normal (necessity or luxury).
a) A 10% decrease in the price of a case of Aviator Lake Beer results in a decrease in total revenue (from beer sales) of 10%.
b) Nikki's Flower Shoppe increases the price of a dozen roses from $10 to $12, but total revenue (from rose sales) remains the same.
c) The price of a box of toothpicks doubles from 30¢ to 60¢ but the quantity purchased does not change.
d) The price of squash racquets increases by 15%, causing the demand for squash balls to decrease by 10%.
e) During the last recession (in which average per capita income was falling), there was an increase in the sales of ground beef for hamburgers.

Problems:
1. Aviator Rylan's Fine Wines of Aviator Lake and its many vineyards have become world renowned. Wine merchants (business travelers) and wine connoisseurs (vacationers) have the following demand for airline tickets from Vancouver or Seattle to Aviator Lake:

Price (return flight)	Quantity Demanded (wine merchants)	Quantity Demanded (wine connoisseurs)
$150	2,100	1,000
$200	2,000	800
$250	1,900	600
$300	1,800	400

a) As the price of tickets rises from $200 to $250, what is the price elasticity of demand for:

8

(i) Wine merchants—business travelers
(ii) Wine connoisseurs—vacationers
    Why might wine connoisseurs have a different elasticity than wine merchants?
b) What ticket price will maximize revenue from wine connoisseurs? What is the price elasticity at this point?
c) Calculate the price elasticity of demand for wine connoisseurs as the price increases from (i) $150 to $200 and (ii) from $250 to $300. Are these elasticities what you would expect given your answers in (b)?

2. The demand curve for Andrea's hand-painted silk scarves is as follows:
    $P = 90 - ¼ Q_D$
    where P is the price one of Andrea's hand-painted silk scarves and Q_D is the quantity of Andrea's hand-painted silk scarves demanded.
a) Calculate the price elasticity of demand when the price decreases from $55 to $50. Is demand elastic, unit elastic, or inelastic?
b) Given the price elasticity calculated in 2 (a), what happens to total revenue when the price of silk decreases from $55 to $50. How do you know? Calculate total revenue when $P = $55 and when $P = $50 to verify your claim.

3. Aviator Ian and Aviator Stu are often found at the LP Café drinking Laura and Petra's wonderful blend of international coffees. Their demand schedule for coffee in cups per year is

Price of coffee	Q_D per year (Income = $70,000) (Price of tea = $1.00)	Q_D per year (Income = $80,000) (Price of tea = $1.00)	Q_D per year (Income = $70,000) (Price of tea = 1.55)
$2.29	600	620	650
$2.45	400	410	420
$2.80	230	240	300

All prices are in dollars per cup.

a) Calculate the cross-price elasticity of demand for coffee with respect to the price of tea if the price of coffee is $2.80 and the income is $70,000. Are coffee and tea substitutes or complements (according to the data)? How do you know?
b) Calculate the income elasticity of demand for coffee if the price of coffee is $2.80 and the price of tea is $1.00. Is coffee a normal or an inferior good (according to the data)? How do you know?

Tutorial #4
Chapter 6: *Markets in Action*

Assignment #4: Price Controls and Taxation

Multiple-Choice Questions:
Choose the one alternative that best completes the statement or answers the question.
1. Consider Figure 4.1. These are four major markets where Aviator Lake Wine is sold. Suppose a sales tax of $1 is imposed. In which market would the buyers bear the highest burden?
a) (a)
b) (b)
c) (c)
d) (d)
e) All markets equally

2. Consider Figure 4.1. These are four major markets where Aviator Lake Wine is sold. Suppose a sales tax of $1 is imposed. In which market would the producer bear the highest burden?
a) (a)
b) (b)
c) (c)
d) (d)
e) All markets equally

Figure 4.1   (a)

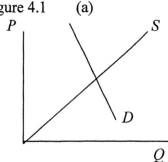

(b)

(c)

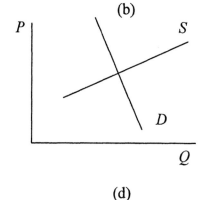

(d)

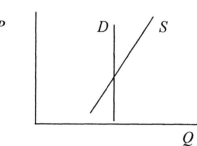

3. If there is a subsidy on the production of wine, the
a) government pays the costs and only producers gain the benefits.
b) government pays the costs and only consumers gain the benefits.
c) consumers pay the costs and producers gain the benefits.
d) producers pay the costs and consumers gain the benefits.
e) government pays the costs and both consumers and producers gain the benefits.

Short-Answer Questions:
1. Aviator Lake Airlines has been consistently losing money on its trans-Pacific flights. To increase revenue, one of the two vice-presidents of the firm has recommended a seat sale (i.e., a decrease in price), whereas the other has recommended increasing the price of the overseas fare. As an economist, explain carefully how you would decide which of the two vice-presidents' advice to accept.

Problems:
1. Aviator Ashleigh owns a large number of cottages on Aviator Lake. The demand and supply curves for two-bedroom cottages in Aviator Lake follow:

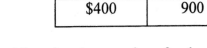

Demand	Demand	New Demand	Supply	New Supply
Price	Quantity	Quantity	Quantity	Quantity
$900			900	
$850	0		800	
$800	100		700	
$750	200		600	
$700	300		500	
$650	400		400	
$600	500		300	
$550	600		200	
$500	700		100	
$450	800		0	
$400	900			

Note that the equations for demand and supply are

Demand: $P = 850 - 0.5Q_D$
Supply: $P = 450 + 0.5Q_S$

a) Using the equations for demand and supply, what is the equilibrium rent per month and the equilibrium quantity of Aviator Ashleigh's Aviator Lake Cottages traded?

b) If a rent ceiling of $500 per month is imposed, what is the quantity of Aviator Ashleigh's Aviator Lake Cottages supplied? What is the quantity of Aviator Ashleigh's Aviator Lake Cottages demanded? Would this create a surplus or a shortage?

c) What is the maximum price that a consumer is willing to pay for the last Aviator Ashleigh's Aviator Lake cottage supplied in part (b)?

d) If the average wage rate of cottage seekers in Aviator Lake is $15 per hour, how many hours per month would a potential renter search for a cottage?

e) Suppose now that Aviator Ashleigh (the landlord) were required to pay $100 per Aviator Lake cottage in a renter's tax to the government of Aviator Lake. Show the new supply schedule for cottages. What is the new equilibrium rent and quantity traded of cottages in Aviator Lake? Write down the new equation for supply.

f) What is the incidence of the tax (i.e., who actually bears the burden of the tax?)?

g) Suppose instead that it is the renters (or buyers) rather than the landlords (or sellers) who are required to pay the $100 tax to the government of Aviator Lake. Show the new demand schedule for cottages. What is the new equilibrium rent and quantity traded of cottages in Aviator Lake? Write down the new equation for demand. Who actually bears the burden of the tax now?

h) How much tax revenue does the government of Aviator Lake collect?

2. The demand for and the supply of grape pickers (labour) in Aviator Lake are as follows:

Wage rate (dollars per hour)	Hours Demanded	Hours Supplied
4	3,000	1,000
5	2,500	1,500
6	2,000	2,000
7	1,500	2,500
8	1,000	3,000

a) What is the equilibrium wage rate in Aviator Lake?

b) What is the level of employment at the equilibrium wage rate in Aviator Lake?

c) What is the level of unemployment at the equilibrium wage rate in Aviator Lake?

d) If the government of Aviator Lake imposes a minimum wage of $5 an hour for grape pickers, how many hours do grape pickers work in Aviator Lake?

e) If the government of Aviator Lake imposes a minimum wage of $7 an hour for grape pickers, what are the employment and unemployment levels in Aviator Lake?

f) If there is a minimum wage of $7 an hour in Aviator Lake and demand increases by 500 hours, what is the level of unemployment in Aviator Lake?

Tutorial #5
Chapter 10: *Output and Costs*

Assignment #5: Production Function and Costs

Multiple-Choice Questions:
Choose the one alternative that best completes the statement or answers the question.
1. When a firm in Aviator Lake operates its plant at capacity or at its efficient point, it is
a) maximizing profits.
b) producing at its physical limits.
c) producing at the level of output at which marginal cost equals average total cost.
d) producing on the upward-sloping part of its long-run average cost curve.

2. When does a firm in Aviator Lake operate its plant at capacity or at its efficient point?
a) If it is maximizing profits
b) If it is producing at its physical limit
c) If it is producing at the level of output at which marginal cost equals average total cost
d) If it is producing on the upward-sloping part of its long-run average cost curve
Note: Question 1 is stated in sentence-completion format, whereas question 2 is the same multiple-choice question, but given in question format.

3. Suppose Aviator Danilo could triple his production of lumber by tripling his production facility for processing logs. This is an example of
a) constant returns to scale.
b) increasing returns to scale.
c) decreasing returns to scale.
d) the law of diminishing returns.
e) economies of scale.

4. What is an example of Aviator Danilo tripling his production of lumber by tripling his production facility for processing logs?
a) Constant returns to scale
b) Increasing returns to scale
c) Decreasing returns to scale
d) The law of diminishing returns
e) Economies of scale
Note: Question 3 is stated in sentence-completion format, whereas question 4 is the same multiple-choice question, but given in question format.

5. The long-run average cost curve for a firm shows
a) the trend in the average cost of a firm over time.
b) the lowest possible average total cost for each level of output when the quantity of all inputs can be changed.
c) the lowest possible average total cost for each level of output when the quantity of some but not all inputs can be changed.
d) the most likely average total cost for each level of output when the quantity of all inputs are changed.

6. What is shown by the long-run average cost curve for a firm?
a) The trend in the average cost of a firm over time
b) The lowest possible average total cost for each level of output when the quantity of all inputs can be changed
c) The lowest possible average total cost for each level of output when the quantity of some but not all inputs can be changed
d) The most likely average total cost for each level of output when the quantity of all inputs are changed

Note: Question 5 is stated in sentence-completion format, whereas question 6 is the same multiple-choice question, but given in question format.

Short-Answer Questions:
1. Define *diminishing marginal returns*.

Problems:
1. The following table shows the monthly output of Aviator Ian's SuperCart Golf Carts (a firm producing very high-powered golf carts) attainable for varying amounts of labour for a given scale of plant as produced by Aviator Ian in Aviator Lake.

Monthly Production of Aviator Ian's SuperCart Golf Carts

Labour Workers/mo.	Output Units/mo.	Marginal Product	Average Product
0	0		
1	1		
2	3		
3	6		
4	12		
5	17		
6	20		
7	22		
8	23		

a) Complete the marginal product and average product columns for Aviator Ian's SuperCart Golf Carts in Aviator Lake. Note that the marginal product figures should be entered midway between successive output figures.

b) Over what range of workers are marginal returns increasing? With the addition of which worker do diminishing marginal returns begin?

14

c) At what level of output does Aviator Ian's marginal product equal the average product? How is the value of the marginal product related to the value of the average product? (If you cannot see this by viewing the data, graph the two curves.)

2. Let us examine the short-run costs of Aviator Ian's SuperCart Golf Carts production in Aviator Lake. The information given in the first two columns of the table in problem 1 is repeated in the first two columns of the following table. Assume that the cost of 1 unit of labour (the only variable input) is $2000 per month and the total fixed cost is $2000 per month.

Short-Run Costs of Aviator Ian's SuperCart Golf Cart production (Monthly, $)

Labour	Output	TFC	TVC	TC	MC	AFC	AVC	ATC
0	0	2000						
1	1							
2	3							
3	6							
4	12							
5	17							
6	20							
7	22							
8	23							

a) Complete the table by calculating total fixed cost (TFC), total variable cost (TVC), total cost (TC), marginal cost (MC) (enter midway between successive output levels), average fixed cost (AFC), average variable cost (AVC), and average total cost (ATC) or (AC).

b) At what level of output does the marginal cost cut the average variable cost curve? What is the relationship between the value of the marginal cost and the value of the average variable cost?

c) At what level of output does diminishing marginal returns set in for Aviator Ian's firm, SuperCart Golf Carts? Does this correspond with your answer to problem 1, part (b)?

d) At what level of output does this firm reach its efficient point? Why? Is the firm at capacity? Is this sometimes called the break-even point? Explain.

e) Are economic profits present? State the value of the profit or loss.

f) What did you notice about the shape of the AVC, ATC, and MC curves?

Tutorial #6
Chapter 11: *Perfect Competition*

Assignment #6: Competition: Price Takers

Multiple-Choice Questions:
Choose the one alternative that best completes the statement or answers the question.
1. Which of the following is *not* a characteristic of a perfectly competitive industry?
a) A downward-sloping industry demand curve
b) A perfectly elastic demand curve for each individual firm
c) Each firm decides its quantity of output
d) Each firm has slightly differentiated products
e) Many firms with each supplying a small fraction of industry supply

2. The characteristic that is *not* present in perfect competition is
a) a downward-sloping industry demand curve.
b) a perfectly elastic demand curve for each individual firm.
c) each firm decides its quantity of output.
d) each firm has slightly differentiated products.
e) many firms with each supplying a small fraction of industry supply.
Note: Question 1 is stated in question format, whereas question 2 is the same multiple-choice
question, but given in sentence-completion format.

3. If economic profits are being made by firms in a competitive industry, new firms will
    enter. In the short run this will shift
a) the industry demand curve leftward, causing market price to fall.
b) the industry demand curve rightward, causing market price to rise.
c) the industry supply curve leftward, causing market price to rise.
d) the industry supply curve rightward, causing market price to fall.
e) none of above curves.

4. If economic profits are being made by firms in a competitive industry and new firms enter,
    what curve will shift in the short run?
a) The industry demand curve leftward, causing market price to fall
b) The industry demand curve rightward, causing market price to rise
c) The industry supply curve leftward, causing market price to rise
d) The industry supply curve rightward, causing market price to fall
e) None of above curves
Note: Question 3 is stated in sentence-completion format, whereas question 4 is the same
multiple-choice question, but given in question format.

5. In a perfectly competitive industry, the market price is $20. An individual firm is producing the output at which $MC = ATC = \$25$. AVC at that output is $20. What should the firm do to maximize its short-run profits?
a) Shut down
b) Expand output
c) Contract output
d) Leave output unchanged
e) Insufficient information to answer

6. When economic profits are zero,
a) the product will not be produced in the short run.
b) the product will not be produced in the long run.
c) firms will leave the industry.
d) revenues are not covering imputed costs.
e) firms are making normal profits.

7. What occurs when economic profits are zero?
a) The product will not be produced in the short run.
b) The product will not be produced in the long run.
c) Firms will leave the industry.
d) Revenues are not covering imputed costs.
e) Firms are making normal profits.
Note: Question 6 is stated in sentence-completion format, whereas question 7 is the same multiple-choice question, but given in question format.

8. The long-run competitive industry supply curve will be positively sloped if there are
a) external economies.
b) external diseconomies.
c) no external economies or diseconomies.
d) external costs.
e) external benefits.

9. When will the long-run competitive industry supply curve will be positively sloped?
a) If there are external economies
b) If there are external diseconomies
c) If there are no external economies or diseconomies
d) If there are external costs
e) If there are external benefits
Note: Question 8 is stated in sentence-completion format, whereas question 9 is the same multiple-choice question, but given in question format.

Short-Answer Questions:
1. The total cost curve for Aaron's Clear Ice Rinks production in Aviator Lake is given as:
$$TC = 3,000 + 60Q + 10Q^2$$
a) Find the total fixed costs and the average fixed costs.

b) Find the total variable costs and the average variable costs.
c) Find the average total costs.

Problems:
1. The following data is for a firm, R&M Brewery that sells its output, premium beer, in a perfectly competitive market. There are four firms in this industry. Assume that the minimum point of the short-run average total cost curve (ATC) is coincident with the minimum point of the long-run average cost curve (LRAC).

Quantity Output	Total Cost	Total Variable Cost	Marginal Cost	Average Cost	Average Variable Cost
0	50	—	—	—	—
			40		
1	90	40		90	40
			30		
2	120	70		60	35
			20		
3	140	90		46.67	30
			30		
4	170	120		42.50	30
			40		
5	210	160		42	32
			50		
6	260	210		43.33	35
			60		
7	320	270		45.71	38.57
			80		
8	400	350		50	43.75

a) If the market price for this premium product is $55 per unit, what is the profit-maximizing output of each firm? Explain. What is the industry output?
b) What is the economic profit/loss of each firm?
c) At approximately what output level would this firm, R&M Brewery, be efficient in the short run?
d) If the market price for the product, premium beer, was $29, how much output would this firm, R&M Brewery, produce?
e) At what output level would this firm shut down in the short run? Explain your answer.
f) Draw a simple graph for the firm, R&M Brewery, showing the market price, profit-maximizing output, break-even point and shut-down point. Label all curves accurately.
g) Construct R&M Brewery's short-run supply curve of output.
h) State the condition for long-run equilibrium of a firm. At what price and output would this firm, R&M Brewery, be in long-run equilibrium?

Tutorial #7
Chapter 12: *Monopoly*

Assignment #7: Market Power: Single-Price Monopoly

Multiple-Choice Questions:
Choose the one alternative that best completes the statement or answers the question.
1. Suppose a monopolist can sell 33 units of output per day for a price of $12 each and 34 units of output per day for $11.75 each. The marginal revenue for the 34th unit sold is equal to
a) $0.
b) $3.50.
c) $11.75.
d) 26 cents.
e) uncertain, as not enough information is given to compute the marginal revenue.

2. Four monopolists were overheard talking at the LP Café. Which one of their statements that follow contains a correct strategy for maximizing profits?
a) "We only increase our output when we know that a greater output will raise total revenue".
b) "Cost minimization is the best way to maximizing profits".
c) "We try to make the most of our equipment by producing at maximum capacity".
d) "I don't continually look at total profits, but I do try to make sure that any new business deals increase my revenue more than they increase my costs".
e) None of the above.

3. A natural monopoly is defined as an industry in which
a) one firm is able to produce the entire industry output at a lower average cost than any other group of firms could.
b) one firm is able to produce the entire industry output at a lower marginal cost than any other group of firms could.
c) one firm is very large relative to other firms entering the industry.
d) a singular firm is able to earn higher profits in an industry than if additional firms enter the same industry.

Short-Answer Questions:
1. Suppose that in the short run, every perfectly competitive firm within an industry was earning economic profits. Using diagrams show the following:
a) What happens to the industry supply curve and, hence, the perfectly competitive market price?
b) What happens to the demand curve facing each and every individual firm?
c) If the short- and long-run average total cost curves are coincident at their minimum points, at what price and output level will each firm (and, hence, the industry as a whole) be in long-run equilibrium? [Hint: It will help you here to state the long-run equilibrium condition.]

Problems:

1. The following diagram shows the cost and revenue information for a monopolist. Aviator Rylan's Fine Wines is the only vineyard and winery on the Island of Aviator Lake.

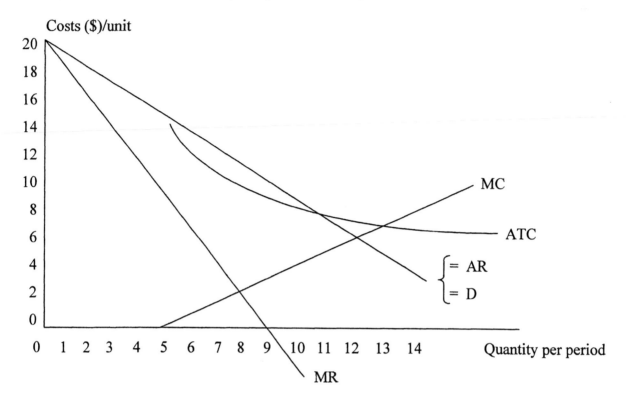

Market for Aviator Rylan's Fine Wines

a) For Aviator Rylan's Fine Wines, a profit-maximizing monopolist, what is the monopoly price? What is the monopoly output?
b) What is the monopoly profit for Aviator Rylan's Fine Wines?
c) At what output would the monopolist, Aviator Rylan's Fine Wines, maximize revenue?
d) Suppose that the market for Aviator Rylan's Fine Wines was organized as a perfectly competitive industry, instead of a monopoly. What would be the perfectly competitive price and industry output? How does it compare to the monopoly price and output?

2. The Pointed Needle Co., run by Melissa and Michal, has the monopoly for making aviator jackets.
   Its demand curve is: $P = 30 - 0.2Q$
   where Q is quantity demanded and P is price per aviator jacket in dollars.
   Its marginal cost curve is: $MC = 6 + 0.6Q$
   where Q is quantity produced per day and MC is marginal cost per aviator jacket in dollars.
   The marginal revenue curve is: $MR = 30 - 0.4Q$
   where Q is quantity sold and MR is marginal revenue per aviator jacket in dollars.
a) Calculate the profit-maximizing price and quantity of aviator jackets for the monopoly that is run by Melissa and Michal.

b) If, instead, the market for aviator jackets was organized as a perfectly competitive industry, what price would be charged for aviator jackets? How many aviator jackets would be produced?

c) Which market structure gives a lower price and a larger output for aviator jackets?

d) Calculate the consumers' surplus when the industry is assumed to be perfectly competitive.

e) Calculate the consumers' surplus portion of the deadweight loss when the industry is assumed to be a monopoly.

3. On the following diagram of a natural monopoly, Rob and Pete's Excellent Mountain Adventures: (1) show marginal cost pricing and label the price P_{eff} and the quantity Q_{eff}, and (2) show average cost pricing and label the price P_{ac} and the quantity Q_{ac}.

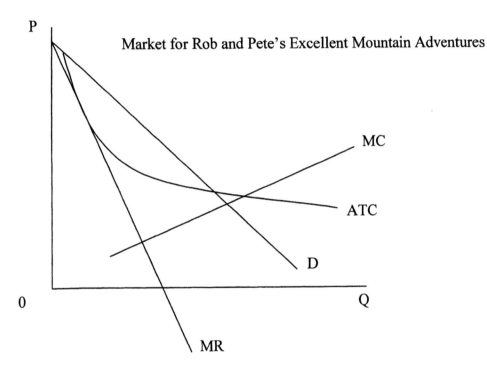

PART FIVE
MARKET FAILURE AND GOVERNMENT

Tutorial #8
Chapter 17: *Demand and Supply in Factor Markets*

Assignment #8: Labour Market

Multiple-Choice Questions:
Choose the one alternative that best completes the statement or answers the question.
1. The marginal revenue product of labour in Aviator Lake is
a) the extra income a worker receives by working an extra hour.
b) the extra profit a firm earns by employing an additional worker.
c) the extra total revenue resulting from hiring one additional worker.
d) the extra output resulting from hiring an additional worker.

2. Which of the following statements is *not* true about the demand for a factor of production in Aviator Lake?
a) It is more elastic when the demand for the final product is more elastic.
b) It is more elastic where technology does not permit substitution with other factors.
c) It is less elastic when the contribution to the total cost of the product is smaller.
d) It is more elastic when a longer time period is considered.

3. As the wage rate increases in Aviator Lake, the substitution effect will give a household an incentive to
a) increase its reservation wage.
b) boost its nonmarket activity and lessen its market activity.
c) boost its market activity and lessen its nonmarket activity.
d) raise both market and nonmarket activities.

4. The income effect of a higher wage rate in Aviator Lake refers to
a) the increase in the workers' purchasing power due to the higher wage rate.
b) the fact that workers need to be paid a higher income if they are to be influenced to work longer hours.
c) the change in the prices of consumer goods that follows higher incomes as wage rates increase.
d) the increase in demand for leisure that is generated by a rise in the wage rate.

5. As the wage rate continues to rise in Aviator Lake, a household will have a backward-bending supply of labour curve if
a) the income effect and the substitution effect are moving in the same direction.
b) the wage rate is higher than the reservation wage.
c) the income effect dominates over the substitution effect.
d) the substitution effect dominates over the income effect.

Short-Answer Questions:

1. Define and draw the marginal revenue product of labour.

2. Define *transfer earnings*. Define *economic rent*.

Problems:

1. You are given the following information about the labour market in the northeastern portion of Aviator Lake. Everyone in this area works for logging companies, but there are many logging companies in the area. The market for logging workers is perfectly competitive and the demand and supply curves for logging workers are as follows:

   Demand: $Q_{DL} = 480 - 40W$

   Supply: $Q_{SL} = 40 + 40W$

   where Q_{SL} = quantity supplied of labour in hours

   Q_{DL} = quantity demanded of labour in hours

   W = wage rate / hour

   a) What is the equilibrium wage rate and quantity of hours employed in the logging industry in Aviator Lake?

   b) What is the total labour income in logging in Aviator Lake?

   c) How much of the labour income in Aviator Lake as found in part (b) is economic rent and how much is transfer earnings?

2. M&M Surf is a small firm run by Melissa and Michal making contoured boogie boards at Brian's Bay on the Island of Aviator Lake. The firm sells its product in a competitive market and buys labour in a competitive market. M&M Surf sells its contoured boogie boards for $150 each, and it has no trouble finding workers willing to work for the market wage of $300 per week.

   a) Complete the MRP_L column in the following table by calculating the marginal revenue product of labour for M&M Surf.

   b) The values obtained for MRP_L will be the same if they are calculated by using either of the following formulas:

   $MRP_L = MP \times MR$

   $MRP_L = \dfrac{\Delta TR}{\Delta L}$

   where MR = marginal revenue of a unit of output

   MP = marginal product of the factor

   ΔTR = change in total revenue from the output

   ΔL = change in the quantity of labour employed

   Show that this is the case when the quantity of labour employed (Petra and Aaron) is two workers per week.

Total Output and Marginal Revenue Product of Labour at M&M Surf

Quantity labour hired/week	Total output /week	MRP_L $ / week
0	0	
1	6	
2	11	
3	15	
4	18	
5	20	
6	21	

Assume: M&M Surf is a profit-maximizing firm.

c) How many workers will M&M Surf employ if the price of contoured boogie boards is $150 each and the market wage is $300 per week? How many contoured boogie boards will the firm produce?

d) Show that at this profit-maximizing level of output, marginal revenue is equal to marginal cost. (Recall that marginal cost can be calculated as the price of the variable factor [labour] divided by the marginal product of the variable factor.)

e) If total fixed cost is $1,000 per week, how much is M&M Surf's profit per week?

f) What will M&M Surf's profit be if the firm employs one more worker each week?

g) Draw a graph of the M&M Surf's demand for labour, showing the supply of labour facing the firm and indicate the quantity of labour employed by the firm.

PART SEVEN
INTERNATIONAL TRADE

Tutorial #9
Chapter 2/32: *Trading with the World*

Assignment #9: Gains from Trade

Multiple-Choice Questions:
Choose the one alternative that best completes the statement or answers the question.
1. In an eight-hour day, Melissa can produce either 24 dozen muffins or 8 cases of jam. In an eight-hour day, Michal can produce either 8 dozen muffins or 8 cases of jam.
a) Melissa has the lower opportunity cost of producing muffins, whereas Melissa and Michal have equal opportunity costs of producing jam.
b) Melissa has the higher opportunity cost of producing both muffins and jam.
c) Melissa has the lower opportunity cost of producing muffins, whereas Michal has the lower opportunity cost of producing jam.
d) Melissa has the lower opportunity cost of producing jam, whereas Michal has the lower opportunity cost of producing muffins.

2. Ashleigh and Adam can produce the following in one week:

Ashleigh		Adam	
Rooms	Cars	Rooms	Cars
8	0	20	0
6	1	15	2
4	2	10	4
2	3	5	6
0	4	0	8

where Rooms is the number of rooms designed and Cars is the number of cars repaired.

Given this information, can Ashleigh and Adam gain by specialization?
a) Yes, unconditionally.
b) No, not under the given circumstances.
c) It depends on the wages each earns.
d) Only if they are married to each other.

3. It pays people to specialize and trade with each other because
a) otherwise they could not survive.
b) they can take advantage of the fact they have an absolute advantage in the production of something.
c) otherwise they cannot sell the food for which they have a higher opportunity cost.
d) they can consume outside their production possibilities frontier.

1. Define *comparative advantage*.

2. Define *absolute advantage*.

Problems:

1. Suppose that two islands, Aviator Lake and Terryland, have the output figures shown in the following table. Two goods are produced: boogie boards and golf clubs.

Average Product per Worker

Country	Boogie Boards	or	Golf Clubs
Aviator Lake	8		4
Terryland	8		6

a) What is the opportunity cost of producing a boogie board in Aviator Lake?
b) What is the opportunity cost of producing a golf club in Aviator Lake?
c) What is the opportunity cost of producing a boogie board in Terryland?
d) What is the opportunity cost of producing a golf club in Terryland?
e) In what product does Aviator Lake have a comparative advantage?
f) In what product does Terryland have a comparative advantage?

g) Suppose that the labour force in Aviator Lake is 5 million, and the labour force is 10 million in Terryland.
   Fill in the missing production possibilities data for both countries in the tables.

Aviator Lake's Production Possibilities (million of units)

	A	B	C	D	E
Boogie Boards	40	30	20	10	0
Golf Clubs					

Terryland's Production Possibilities (millions of units)

	A	B	C	D	E
Boogie Boards					
Golf Clubs	0	15	30	45	60

h) Suppose that both countries are presently producing at combination D.
Show the joint totals before trade in the following table:

Total Output in Millions of Units

	Boogie Boards	Golf Clubs
Aviator Lake		
Terryland		
Total: Both countries		

i) Now suppose that each country specializes in the product in which it has a comparative advantage. Show the new totals after trade in the following table:

Total Output in Millions of Units

	Boogie Boards	Golf Clubs
Aviator Lake		
Terryland		
Total: Both countries		

j) As a result, the joint gain from trade is equal to:

_____ boogie boards, _____ golf clubs.

Assignment Answers

Tutorial #1
Chapter 2: *The Economics Problem*

Assignment #1: Production Possibilities and Opportunity Cost

Multiple-Choice Questions:
1. The Aviator Lake Music Company makes compact disc players and compact discs. The following table summarizes its production capacity.

Points on Aviator Lake Music Company's PPF

Point	Production of Players (number/day)	Production of Discs (number/day)
a	0	400
b	4	360
c	8	280
d	12	160
e	16	0

Use this information to answer the following question.
Aviator Lake Music Company produces 8 players and 280 discs per day and will be increasing its daily player production to 12. The table shows that each additional player will cost: [c]
a) 160 discs
b) 120 discs
c) 30 discs
d) 13.3 discs

2. A situation in which all resources in Aviator Lake Music Company are *not* fully utilized is represented in a production possibility frontier diagram by   [d]
a) any point on either the horizontal or vertical axis.
b) a point above or to the right of the production possibility frontier.
c) a point outside the production possibility frontier.
d) a point inside the production possibility frontier.

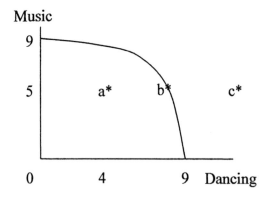

There are two goods: music and dancing. The next two questions refer to this diagram.

3. Refer to the preceding production possibility frontier. Which of the following is true about point a? [c]
a) It is unattainable.
b) Although no more music can be produced, more dancing can be produced.
c) Resources are not fully employed.
d) It is preferred to point b.

4. In the preceding diagram, [b]
a) movement from point a to point b would require a technological improvement.
b) point b is superior to point a.
c) some resources must be unemployed at point c.
d) the concept of decreasing opportunity cost is illustrated.

Short-Answer Questions:
1. There is an expression: 'You can't have your cake and eat it too'. Explain carefully which economic concept is illustrated in this statement and what it means.
The expression illustrates the concept of opportunity cost. Opportunity cost is the best alternative foregone. The concept illustrates what is meant by eating your cake (i.e., use it to satisfy hunger), the opportunity cost is not having it. You cannot have it both ways. The cost of any action is the alternative foregone.
2. Are the following statements positive or normative? Explain.
i) Aviator Stu, the Governor of the Central Bank of Aviator Lake sets the interest rate at 4%. This is a positive statement. It is a factual statement and tells us what is, was, or will be. It is a statement which can be tested.
ii) Aviator Ashleigh thinks the Central Bank of Aviator Lake should set its interest rate at 3.5%. This is a normative statement. It is not factual and it cannot be tested,

Problems:
1. Fog has rolled in on Aviator Lake, and all planes are grounded. Aviator Ashleigh is planning how to spend this foggy Sunday, and the choice is between watching DVDs (each lasting 2 hours) or studying her microeconomics textbook. She has 10 hours available to her. If she decides to study, she could read the following number of pages:

2 hours	80 pages
4 hours	130 pages
6 hours	160 pages
8 hours	175 pages
10 hours	180 pages

**Note: Scarcity:
- Limited amount of time in hours/day [resources]

Choice:
- Watch videos or study economics

Opportunity cost:
- Incurred

31

Hours	Microeconomics pages	or	DVDs
2	80		1
4	130		2
6	160		3
8	175		4
10	180		5

Number of hours available = 10

All Microeconomics   ⇨   read 180 pages
or All DVDs   ⇨   watch 5

Microeconomics pages

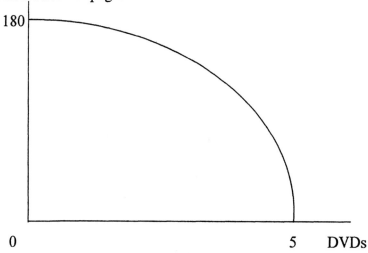

a) Given this information, draw Aviator Ashleigh's production possibility curve between DVDs watched and pages of microeconomics studied.

Point	Microeconomics Pages	Videos
A	180	0
B	175	1
C	160	2
D	130	3
E	80	4
F	0	5

**Note: The label 'Microeconomics pages' could be placed on either axis. It does not matter.

Microeconomics pages

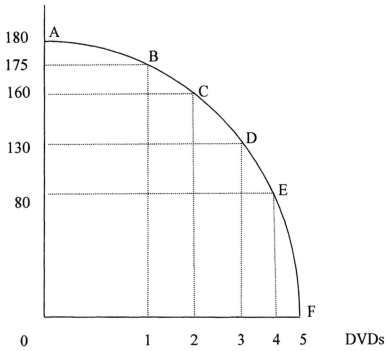

b) What happens to the opportunity cost of watching DVDs as more DVDs are watched? (Support your answer with calculations.)

<u>From Point A to Point B:</u>
1 video opportunity cost = $\dfrac{\text{give up}}{\text{get}}$ = $\left| \dfrac{180 - 175}{0 - 1} \right|$ = $\dfrac{5}{1}$ = 5 microeconomics pages.

<u>From Point B to Point C:</u>
1 video opportunity cost = $\left| \dfrac{175 - 160}{1 - 2} \right|$ = $\dfrac{15}{1}$ = 15 microeconomics pages.

<u>From Point C to Point D:</u>
1 video opportunity cost = $\left| \dfrac{160 - 130}{2 - 3} \right|$ = $\dfrac{30}{1}$ = 30 microeconomics pages.

<u>From Point D to Point E:</u>
1 video opportunity cost = $\left| \dfrac{130 - 80}{3 - 4} \right|$ = $\dfrac{50}{1}$ = 50 microeconomics pages.

<u>From Point E to Point F:</u>
1 video opportunity cost = $\left| \dfrac{80 - 0}{4 - 5} \right|$ = $\dfrac{80}{1}$ = 80 microeconomics pages.

<u>Opportunity Costs Increase:</u>
The number of DVDs watched increases as more pages of microeconomics are given up.

c) Could Aviator Ashleigh watch 3 DVDs and study 150 pages of her textbook? Explain.

Microeconomics pages   DVDs & 150 pages Microeconomics?

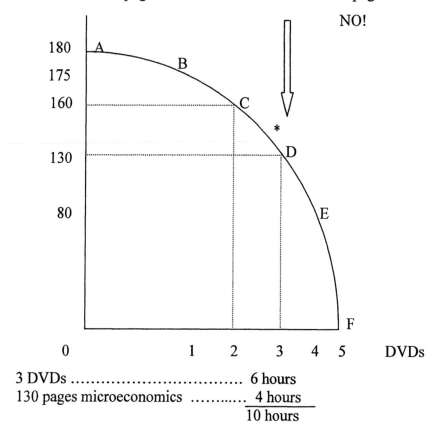

NO!

3 DVDs .... 6 hours
130 pages microeconomics .... 4 hours
                                     _____
                                     10 hours

   i)   To watch 3 DVDs and read 150 pages of microeconomics is outside the production possibility frontier.
   ii) Insufficient resources to achieve this level.

d) If Aviator Ashleigh has already read 160 pages, what is the opportunity cost of reading 1 more page? What is the opportunity cost of reading 15 more pages?
   ▪ At point C
   ▪ Watching 2 DVDs
   ▪ Moving to point B
   ▪ Moving up the vertical axis
   ▪ Wants to read more microeconomics
   ▪ Opportunity cost = $\frac{\text{give up}}{\text{get}}$

From Point C to Point B:

1 more microeconomics page opportunity cost = $\left| \frac{2-1}{160-175} \right| = \frac{1}{15} = 0.067$ DVD

15 more microeconomics pages opportunity cost = [15 * 0.067] or, [15 * $\frac{1}{15}$] = 1 DVD

   ** [when at Point C]

34

Microeconomics pages

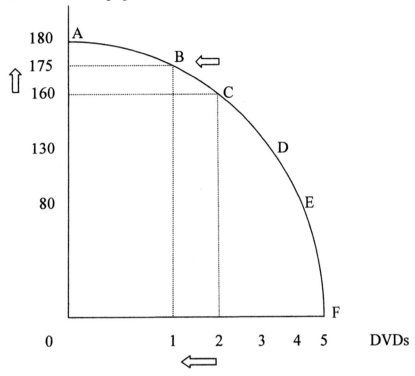

c) If Aviator Ashleigh takes a speed-reading course, show the effect on her production possibility curve.

- No change in her ability to watch DVDs
- Production Possibilities Curve rotates rightward [or outwardly] only on the y-axis (Microeconomics)
- Aviator Ashleigh's ability to read more pages each and every hour has increased
- Two hundred [200] was a randomly chosen number higher than the original intercept of 180

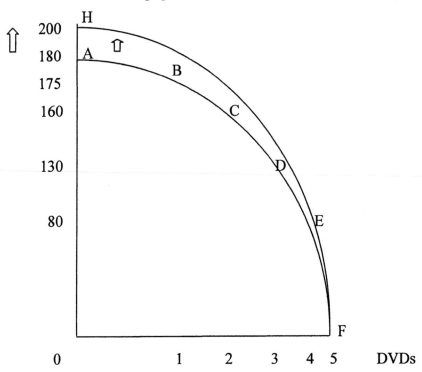

Tutorial #2
Chapter 3: *Demand and Supply*

Assignment #2: Demand and Supply Determinants, Schedules, Graphs, and Equations

Multiple-Choice Questions:

1. If the price of oil in Aviator Lake, a close substitute for Alberta's coal, increases, then [b]
a) the supply curve for Alberta coal will shift to the right.
b) the demand curve for Alberta coal will shift to the right.
c) the equilibrium price and quantity of Alberta coal will not change.
d) the quantity of Alberta coal demanded will decline.

Short-Answer Questions:
1. If we observe a decrease in the price of computers in Aviator Lake and an increase in quantity traded, then we know that the supply of computers has increased. True/false? Explain.

Market for Computers in Aviator Lake

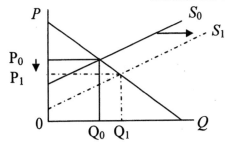

An increase in supply will cause the price of computers to decrease and the quantity demanded of computers to increase. We know this statement to be true.

2. What effect will the following have on the demand, supply, price, and quantity traded of Aviator Rylan's Fine Wines in Aviator Lake?
a) The number of wineries increases.

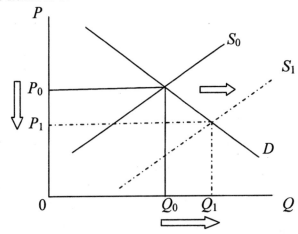

Market for Aviator Rylan's Fine Wines

- Supply increases
- Supply curve shifts rightward
- Price decreases
- Quantity demanded increases

b) The price of beer increases.

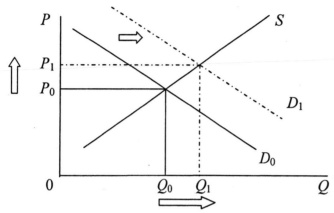

Market for Aviator Rylan's Fine Wines

- Beer and wine are *substitutes*
- As the price of beer increases, the quantity demanded of beer decreases
- Demand for Aviator Rylan's Fine Wines increase
- Demand curve shifts rightward
- Price of wine increases
- Quantity supplied of wine increases

c) A bad harvest occurs in the grape industry.

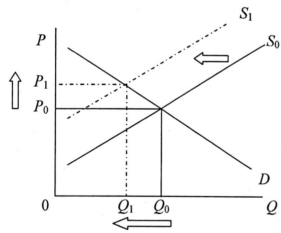

Market for Aviator Rylan's Fine Wines

- Grapes are a factor of production [resource]
- Fewer grapes available & more expensive
- Supply for Aviator Lake Wine decreases

- Supply shifts leftward
- Price increases
- Quantity demanded decreases

d) High winds and hailstorms rage through Aviator Lake. At the same time, more people are purchasing greater quantities of Aviator Rylan's Fine Wines.

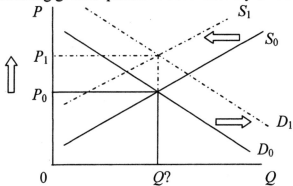

Market for Aviator Rylan's Fine Wines

- Increase in the price of a factor of production
- Supply decreases, shifts leftward
- Increased demand for Aviator Lake wine
- Demand increases, shifts rightward
- Price increases
- Quantity is ambiguous

3. Correct the following statements, if needed, so that there is correct usage of the terms "demand", "quantity demanded", "supply", and "quantity supplied".

a) As the price of Aviator Rylan's Fine Wines in Aviator Lake increases, consumers demand less Aviator Rylan's Fine Wine.

[incorrect]

As the price of Aviator Rylan's Fine Wine increases, quantity demanded of Aviator Rylan's Fine Wines is less.

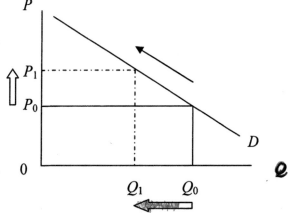

Market for Aviator Rylan's Fine Wines

- Movement along the demand curve
- Change in prices never shift a curve

b) An increase in incomes of scooter buyers will increase the quantity demanded for scooters in Aviator Lake.   [incorrect]
An increase in incomes of scooter buyers will increase the demand for scooters in Aviator Lake.

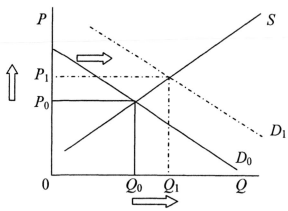

Market for Scooters in Aviator Lake

- Scooters are a normal good
- When incomes increase, demand for normal goods increase
- Demand shifts rightward
- Price increases
- Quantity supplied increases

c) A decrease in the supply of fish means suppliers will provide fewer fish—whatever the current price is.   [correct]
A decrease in the supply of fish means suppliers will provide fewer fish at each and every price level.

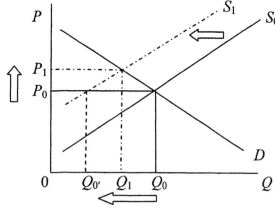

Market for Aviator Lake Fish

40

- Supply decreases, so fewer fish are supplied at each and every price (including the current price)
- Supply shifts leftward
- Prices increase
- Quantity demanded decreases

d) The price of bicycles-built-for-two in Aviator Lake increases if the supply of bicycles-built-for-two in Aviator Lake decreases.   [correct]

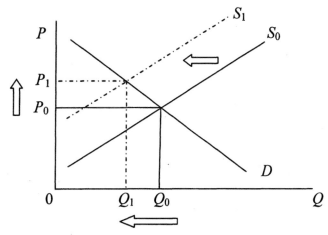

Market for bicycles-built-for-two in Aviator Lake

- Supply decreases
- Supply shifts leftward
- Prices increase
- Quantity demanded decreases

4. An increase in the price of Aviator Lake Honey raises the price of sugar and increases the quantity of sugar traded. Therefore, sugar and Aviator Lake Honey are substitutes. True/false? Explain.

When the price of Aviator Lake Honey increases, the quantity demanded of Aviator Lake Honey will decline; residents of Aviator Lake will now look for a cheaper alternative, sugar. Sugar and Aviator Lake Honey are substitutes. Assuming a normal upward-sloping supply curve, the demand for sugar will increase, causing both the price and quantity traded (or, quantity supplied) of sugar to increase. This statement is true.

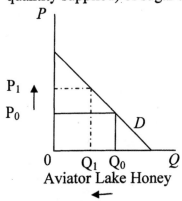

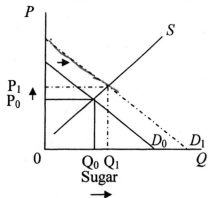

5. Technological innovations in the production of computers in Aviator Lake make the firms more productive. True/false? Explain.

An increase in technology increases supply. The supply curve shifts rightward, moves along a downward-sloping demand curve causing prices to decrease and quantity traded (or, quantity demanded) to increase. Aviator Lake is now producing more computers at a cheaper price; computer firms in Aviator Lake are more productive. This statement is true.

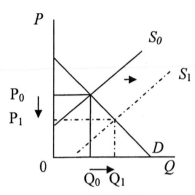

Aviator Lake Computers

Problems:

1. Suppose that the supply and demand for Nikki's Aviator Lake Strawberries in the Nunavut market are as follows (the quantities are in thousands of kilos per week):

Price	Quantity Demanded	Quantity Supplied
$4.00	140	60
4.25	130	70
4.50	120	80
4.75	110	90
5.00	100	100
5.25	90	110
5.50	80	120

a) What are the equilibrium price and quantity of Nikki's Aviator Lake Strawberries in Nunavut?

In equilibrium, demand = supply or, quantity demanded = quantity supplied

or, $Q_D = Q_S = Q^*$

$Q^* = 100$ thousand kilos per week [or, 100,000]

$P^* = \$5$

b) The demand and supply equations for the preceding data are as follows:

$Q_D = 300 - 40P$ Inverse demand curve: $[P = 7.5 - 0.025\ Q_D]$

$Q_S = -100 + 40P$ $[P = 2.5 + 0.025\ Q_S]$

Solve the equations for equilibrium P and Q as a check on you answer in (a).

42

In equilibrium $Q_D = Q_S = Q^*$

$-100 + 40P = 300 - 40P$

$40P + 40P = 300 + 100$

$80P = 400$

$P = 400 / 80$

$P^* = \$5$

Substitute P = 5 in either demand or supply. Here it is demand.

$Q = 300 - 40 (5)$

$Q = 300 - 200$

$Q^* = 100$ thousand kilos per week

- -

In equilibrium $Q_D = Q_S = Q^*$ [using the inverse equations]

$2.5 + 0.025\ Q = 7.5 - 0.025\ Q$

$0.025\ Q + 0.025\ Q = 7.5 - 2.5$

$0.05\ Q = 5$

$Q^* = 100$ thousand kilos per week

Substitute $Q = 100$ in Supply

$P = 2.5 + 0.025 (100)$

$P = 2.5 + 2.5$

$P^* = \$5$

c) Use the equations to find the intercepts of the demand and supply curves for Nikki's Aviator Lake Strawberries. Plot the supply and demand curves for Nikki's Aviator Lake Strawberries showing the intercepts and the equilibrium price and quantity.

General equation of a straight line $Y = m\,X + b$

Slope   intercept

Demand: $P = 7.5 - 0.025\ Q_D$

When $Q_D = 0$

$P = 7.5$ Y-axis intercept

$Q_D = 300 - 40P$

$0 = 300 - 40P$

$40P = 300$

$P = 300 / 40$

$P = \$7.5$

When $P = 0$

$Q_D = 300$ X-axis intercept

$Q_D = 300 - 40P$

$Q_D = 300 - 40 (0)$

$Q_D = 300$ thousand kilos per week   [or, 300,000]

43

Supply: $Q_S = -100 + 40P$

When $P = 0$
         $Q_S = -100$ $X-$ axis intercept   [or, $-100,000$]

When $Q = 0$
         $P = \$2.5$ Y-axis intercept

d) Suppose there is an increase in demand for Nikki's Aviator Lake Strawberries such that the equation for demand is now:
   $Q_D' = 380 - 40P$
   What is the new equilibrium price and quantity traded?

   Demand Increases: $Q_D' = 380 - 40P$
                        $Q_S = -100 + 40P$
   In equilibrium $Q_D' = Q_S = Q'^*$
        $-100 + 40P = 380 - 40P$
        $40P + 40P = 380 + 100$
             $80P = 480$
              $P = 480 / 80$
             $P'^* = \$6$

   Substitute $P'^* = 6$ into Supply or Demand
        $Q = 380 - 40 (6)$
        $Q = 380 - 240$
        $Q'^* = 140$ thousand kilos per week   [or, $140,000$]

   New Intercepts:
   When $Q_D' = 0$
                        $Q_D' = 380 - 40P$
                         $0 = 380 - 40P$
                     $40P = 380$
                      $P = 380 / 40$
                      $P = \$9.5$ Y-axis intercept
   When $P = 0$
   $Q_D' = 380 - 40P$
   $Q_D' = 380$ X-axis intercept   [or, $380,000$]

44

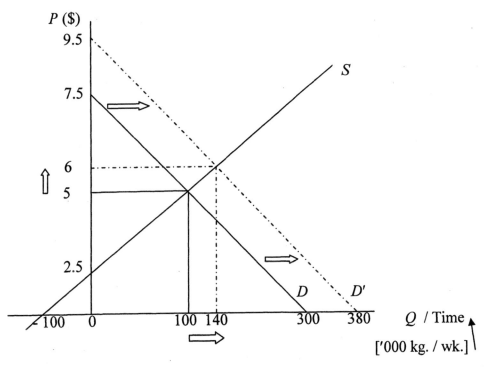

P ($)

Market for Nikki's Aviator Lake Strawberries

2. Suppose that Aviator Adam's Flying School students' demand for Aerodrome concert tickets is as follows:

Price	Quantity Demanded	Quantity Supplied	Q_D'
$ 6.00	8,000	5,000	16,000
8.00	5,000	5,000	10,000
9.00	2,500	5,000	5,000
10.00	1,500	5,000	3,000
11.00	1,000	5,000	2,000

Concert pricing policy is set by Aviator Adam, who has decided that all seats will sell at the same price regardless of location or popularity of the performer (clearly, Aviator Adam is a mechanical engineer and not an economist). Also, the only concert hall available is Aerodrome, and it has a seating capacity of 5,000.

a) If Aviator Adam sets a price of $10 per seat, is there an excess demand or supply of concert tickets in Aviator Lake?

$P = \$10$
$Q_D = 1,500$ $Q_S = 5,000$
$Q_S > Q_D$ excess supply of 3,500 seats

b) What price would fill the Aerodrome concert hall without creating a shortage of seats?
In equilibrium $Q_D = Q_S = Q^* = 5,000$
$$P^* = \$8$$

45

c) Suppose the preceding demand schedule refers to an "average" concert, and when a particularly popular performer is booked, the quantity of tickets demanded at each price doubles. What would be the equilibrium ticket price for a popular performer at the Aerodrome?

First determine Q_D' e.g. at $6.00 $Q_D = 8000$ $Q_D' = [8,000 (2)] = 16,000$
In equilibrium $Q_D = Q_S = Q^* = 5,000$
$$P^* = \$9$$

d) Do you think ticket scalping would be more profitable if the price were set equal to, above, or below equilibrium? Explain.

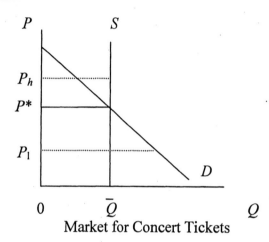

Market for Concert Tickets

P_h: at higher price $Q_S > Q_D$ [above equilibrium]
P^*: at equilibrium $Q_S = Q_D$
P_l: at lower price $Q_S < Q_D$ [below equilibrium]
If the price were lower than equilibrium, there would be excess demand, and scalping would be more profitable.

Tutorial #3
Chapter 4: *Elasticity*

Assignment #3: Elasticity, Determinants, and Equations

Multiple-Choice Questions:
1. If the price elasticity of demand for Aviator Lake Beer is 2 and price increases by 2%, the quantity demanded [a]
   a) decreases by 4%.
   b) decreases by 1%.
   c) decreases by 2%.
   d) cannot be determined with this information.

2. Michal allocates $200 for her monthly expenditure on compact discs and decides to spend no more and no less, regardless of price. Michal's demand for compact discs is [c]
   a) perfectly inelastic.
   b) perfectly elastic.
   c) unit elasticity.
   d) less than one but greater than zero.

3. Which of the following is more likely to have an elastic demand? [c]
   a) Sea salt
   b) Rye bread
   c) Beef steak
   d) 1% milk

4. Which of the following pairs of commodities is likely to have a cross-price elasticity of demand that is positive? [c]
   a) Hockey sticks and pucks
   b) Rye bread and cheddar cheese
   c) Tapes and compact discs
   d) French perfume and garden hose

5. If the price elasticity of supply of blueberries in Aviator Lake is 0.1, this means that a [b]
   a) 0.1% increase in price is matched by a 0.1% increase in quantity supplied.
   b) 10% decrease in price is associated with a 1% decrease in quantity supplied.
   c) 10% increase in price will increase total revenue by 0.1%.
   d) 1% decrease in price induces a 10% decrease in quantity supplied.

6. To avoid an increase in the local property tax, Aviator Ashleigh, who is the owner of Aviator Lake Cottages, proposes a 2% lodging tax. It is assumed that this tax would be shifted to tourists. The hotel/cottage rental industry owners argue that the tax would hurt business because tourists would go elsewhere. What the hotel/cabin owners were really saying is that [b]

a) tourist demand is inelastic, so the tax would be passed onto the tourists.
b) tourist demand is very elastic, so hotels and cabins would have to bear the tax.
c) they would prefer a property-tax increase.
d) it is unfair to tax people who do not live in the area.

7. A necessity is [a]
a) a normal good with an income elasticity that is less than one.
b) an inferior good.
c) a normal good with an income elasticity that is greater than one.
d) a normal good with an income elasticity of less than zero.

Short-Answer Questions:

1. In each of the following scenarios in Aviator Lake, indicate whether the event deals with own-price elasticity, cross-price elasticity, or income elasticity. If own-price elasticity, indicate whether demand is elastic, inelastic, or unit elastic; if cross-price elasticity, indicate whether the goods are complements or substitutes; if income elasticity, indicate whether the good is inferior or normal (necessity or luxury).

a) A 10% decrease in the price of a case of Aviator Lake Beer results in a decrease in total revenue (from beer sales) of 10%.

$P \downarrow \rightarrow TR \downarrow$ $\eta d < 1$ Inelastic

b) Nikki's Flower Shoppe increases the price of a dozen roses from $10 to $12, but total revenue (from rose sales) remains the same.

$P \uparrow \rightarrow \overline{TR}$ $\eta d = 1$ Unit Elastic

c) The price of a box of toothpicks doubles from 30¢ to 60¢ but the quantity purchased does not change.

$\overline{Q}^D / 2*P \uparrow$ $\eta d < 1$ Perfectly Inelastic
very small portion of budget

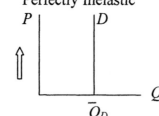

d) The price of squash racquets increases by 15%, causing the demand for squash balls to decrease by 10%.

$- 10\% \Delta Q^D \downarrow$ balls $/ + 15\% \Delta P \uparrow$ squash racquets [–] Complements
Cross-Price Elasticity

e) During the last recession (in which average per capita income was falling) there was an increase in the sales of ground beef for hamburgers.

$+ \% \Delta Q^D \uparrow$ ground beef $/ - \% \Delta I \downarrow$ Income [–] Inferior good
Income Elasticity

48

Problems:

1. Aviator Rylan's Fine Wines of Aviator Lake and its many vineyards have become world renowned. Wine merchants (business travelers) and wine connoisseurs (vacationers) have the following demand for airline tickets from Vancouver or Seattle to Aviator Lake:

Price (return)	Quantity Demanded (wine merchants)	Quantity Demanded (wine connoisseurs)
$150	2,100	1,000
$200	2,000	800
$250	1,900	600
$300	1,800	400

a) As the price of tickets rises from $200 to $250, what is the price elasticity of demand for:
   (i) Wine merchants—business travelers
   (ii) Wine connoisseurs—vacationers
   (iii) Why might wine connoisseurs have a different elasticity than wine merchants?

$$\eta d = \frac{\% \, \Delta Q_D}{\% \, \Delta P}$$

(i) <u>Wine merchants:</u>

$$\eta d = \frac{\dfrac{2000 - 1900}{[2000 + 1900] / 2}}{\dfrac{200 - 250}{[200 + 250] / 2}}$$

$$= \frac{\dfrac{100}{1950}}{\dfrac{-50}{225}} \qquad = \frac{0.051}{-0.222}$$

$$= \left| -0.2297 \right| \qquad = 0.23$$

$\eta d < 1$ Inelastic

(ii) <u>Wine connoisseurs:</u>

$$\eta d = \frac{\dfrac{800 - 600}{[800 + 600] / 2}}{\dfrac{200 - 250}{[200 + 250] / 2}}$$

$$= \frac{\dfrac{200}{700}}{\dfrac{-50}{225}} \qquad = \frac{0.286}{-0.222}$$

$$= \left| -1.288 \right| \qquad = 1.29$$

$\eta d > 1$ Elastic

- Because of time constraints, there are fewer alternatives for wine merchants.
- Demand is more inelastic.

b) What ticket price will maximize revenue from wine connoisseurs? What is the price elasticity at this point?

Wine connoisseurs:
- Ticket price to maximize revenue

- Where $\eta d = 1$
- Unit elastic

- $P \times Q = TR$ at $\eta d = 1$ then TR is maximized
- $[(P = 200)(Q = 800)] = \$160,000$

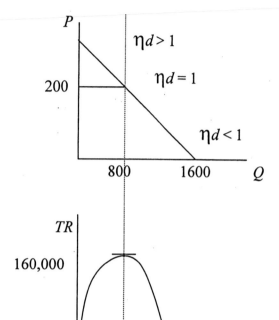

c) Calculate the price elasticity of demand for wine connoisseurs as the price increases from (i) $150 to $200 and (ii) from $250 to $300. Are these elasticities what you would expect given your answers in (b)?

Wine connoisseurs: $\eta d = \dfrac{\% \Delta Q_D}{\% \Delta P}$

(i)

$$\eta d = \dfrac{\dfrac{1000 - 800}{[1000 + 800] / 2}}{\dfrac{150 - 200}{[150 + 200] / 2}}$$

50

$$= \frac{\dfrac{200}{900}}{\dfrac{-50}{175}}$$

$$= \frac{0.222}{-0.286}$$

$$= \left| -0.776 \right|$$

consistent with diagram

$$= 0.78$$

$\eta_d < 1$ Inelastic

(ii)

$$\eta_d = \frac{\dfrac{600 - 400}{[600 + 400]/2}}{\dfrac{250 - 300}{[250 + 300]/2}}$$

$$= \frac{\dfrac{200}{500}}{\dfrac{-50}{275}}$$

$$= \frac{0.4}{-0.182}$$

$$= \left| -2.197 \right|$$

$$= 2.2$$

$\eta_d > 1$ Elastic

2. The demand curve for Andrea's hand-painted silk scarves is as follows:
   $P = 90 - \frac{1}{4} Q_D$
   where P is the price one of Andrea's hand-painted silk scarves and Q_D is the quantity of Andrea's hand-painted silk scarves demanded.

a) Calculate the price elasticity of demand when the price decreases from \$55 to \$50. Is demand elastic, unit elastic, or inelastic?
   - Demand curve for Andrea's hand-painted silk scarves: $P = 90 - \frac{1}{4} Q_D$
   - Income = \$40,000
   - Price of Andrea's hand-painted silk scarves $\downarrow$ from \$55 to \$50

   $P = \$55$ $55 = 90 - \frac{1}{4} Q_D$
                         $\frac{1}{4} Q_D = 90 - 55$
                              $Q_D = 35 / 1/4$
                              $Q_D = 35 \, (4/1)$
                              $Q_D = 140$

$P' = \$50$

$$50 = 90 - 1/4 \; Q_D$$
$$1/4 \; Q_D = 90 - 50$$
$$Q_D = 40 \; (4/1)$$
$$Q_D' = 160$$

$$\eta d = \frac{\% \; \Delta Q_D}{\% \; \Delta P}$$

$$\eta d = \frac{\dfrac{140 - 160}{[140 + 160\;]/2}}{\dfrac{55 - 50}{[55 + 50]/2}}$$

$$= \frac{\dfrac{-20}{150}}{\dfrac{5}{52.5}}$$

$$= \frac{-0.133}{0.095}$$

$$= \left| \; -1.4 \; \right|$$

$$= 1.4$$

$$\eta d > 1 \qquad \text{Elastic}$$

b) Given the price elasticity calculated in 2 (a), what happens to total revenue when the price of silk decreases from $55 to $50. How do you know? Calculate total revenue when $P = \$55$ and when $P = \$50$ to verify your claim.

If $P \downarrow$ and $\eta d > 1$ Elastic, then $TR \uparrow$

In the elastic region, when the price decreases [$P \downarrow$], total revenue [$TR \uparrow$].
Because demand is elastic, the percentage increase in quantity sold is greater than the percentage decrease in price. Total revenue increases when price falls because the quantity sold has increased more.

$$P \; x \; Q = TR$$
1. $\$55 \; (140) = \$7,700$
2. $\$50 \; (160) = \$8,000$

3. Aviator Ian and Aviator Stu are often found at the LP Café drinking Laura and Petra's wonderful blend of international coffees. Their demand schedule for coffee in cups per year is

Price of coffee	Q_D per year (Income = $70,000) (Price of tea = 1.00)	Q_D per year (Income = $80,000) (Price of tea = 1.00)	Q_D per year (Income = $70,000) (Price of tea = 1.55)
$2.29	600	620	650
$2.45	400	410	420
$2.80	230	240	300

All prices are dollars per cup.

a) Calculate the cross-price elasticity of demand for coffee with respect to the price of tea if the price of coffee is $2.80 and the income is $70,000. Are coffee and tea substitutes or complements (according to the data)? How do you know?
- You may use the new – old
- Or, you can keep the price of tea and the Q_D of coffee from the same column together in either the first or secondary position

Price of coffee = $2.80 constant
Income = $70,000 constant
Q_D of coffee ↑ from 230 to 300
Price of tea ↑ from $1.00 to $1.55

$$\eta_{c,t} = \frac{\% \,\Delta\, Q_D \text{ Coffee}}{\% \,\Delta\, P \text{ Tea}}$$

$$\eta_{c,t} = \frac{\dfrac{300 - 230}{[300 + 230]/2}}{\dfrac{1.55 - 1.00}{[1.55 + 1.00]/2}}$$

$$= \frac{\dfrac{70}{265}}{\dfrac{0.55}{1.275}}$$

$$= \frac{0.264}{0.431}$$

$$\eta_{c,t} = +0.612$$

$$\eta_{c,t} > 0 \quad \text{Positive} \quad \text{Substitute}$$

They are substitutes because the cross-price elasticity of demand is positive.
An increase in the price of tea results in an increase in the demand for coffee, ceteris paribus.

b) Calculate the income elasticity of demand for coffee if the price of coffee is $2.80 and the price of tea is $1.00. Is coffee a normal or an inferior good (according to the data)? How do you know?

Price of coffee	Q_D per year, coffee (Income = $70,000) (Price of tea = 1.00)	Q_D per year, coffee (Income = $80,000) (Price of tea = 1.00)	Q_D per year, coffee (Income = $70,000) (Price of tea = 1.55)
$2.29	600	620	650
$2.45	400	410	420
$2.80	230	240	300

Price of coffee = $2.80 constant
Price of tea = $1.00 constant
Income ↑ from $70,000 to $80,000
Q_D of coffee ↑ from 230 to 240

$$\eta_I = \frac{\% \, \Delta Q_D}{\% \, \Delta I}$$

$$\eta_I = \frac{\dfrac{240 - 230}{[240 + 230] / 2}}{\dfrac{80,000 - 70,000}{[80,000 + 70,000] / 2}}$$

$$= \frac{\dfrac{10}{235}}{\dfrac{10,000}{75,000}}$$

$$= \frac{0.043}{0.133}$$

$$\eta_I = +0.323$$

$\eta_I > 0$ \qquad Positive \qquad Normal Good

Coffee is a normal good because the income elasticity is positive. An increase in income will result in an increase in the demand for coffee, ceteris paribus.

Because $\eta_I > 0 < 1$, coffee is a normal good that is income inelastic.

Tutorial #4
Chapter 6: *Markets in Action*

Assignment #4: Price Controls and Taxation

Multiple-Choice Questions:
1. Consider Figure 4.1. These are four major markets where Aviator Lake Wine is sold. Suppose a sales tax of $1 is imposed. In which market would the buyer bear the highest burden?   [d]
a) (a)
b) (b)
c) (c)
d) (d)
e) All markets equally

2. Consider Figure 4.1. These are four major markets where Aviator Lake Wine is sold. Suppose a sales tax of $1 is imposed. In which market would the seller bear the highest burden?   [c]
a) (a)
b) (b)
c) (c)
d) (d)
e) All markets equally

Figure 4.1   (a)

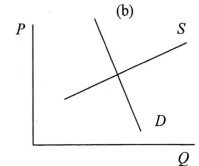

(b)

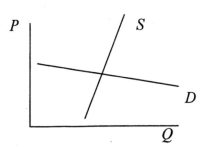

(c)

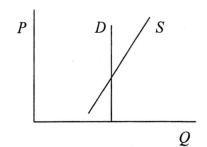

(d)

55

3. If there is a subsidy on the production of a good, the [e]
a) government pays the costs and only producers gain the benefits.
b) government pays the costs and only consumers gain the benefits.
c) consumers pay the costs and producers gain the benefits.
d) producers pay the costs and consumers gain the benefits.
e) government pays the costs and both consumers and producers gain the benefits.

Short-Answer Questions:
1. Aviator Lake Airlines has been consistently losing money on its trans-Pacific flights. To increase revenue, one of the two vice-presidents of the firm has recommended a seat sale (i.e., a decrease in price), whereas the other has recommended increasing the price of the overseas fare. As an economist, explain carefully how you would decide which of the two vice-presidents' advice to accept.
To decide, we need to know something about the elasticity of demand in the relevant price range. If demand is elastic, a decrease in price would increase revenue, but, if demand is inelastic, an increase in price would increase revenue.

Problems:
1. Aviator Ashleigh owns a large number of cottages on Aviator Lake. The demand and supply curves for two-bedroom cottages in Aviator Lake follow:

Demand	Demand	New Demand	Supply	New Supply
Price	Quantity	Quantity	Quantity	Quantity
$900			900	700
$850	0		800	600
$800	100		700	500
$750	200	0	600	400
$700	**300**	100	500	**300**
$650	**400**	200	**400**	200
$600	500	300	300	100
$550	600	400	200	0
$500	700	500	100	
$450	800	600	0	
$400	900	700		

Note that the equations for demand and supply are

Demand: $P = 850 - 0.5Q_D$
Supply: $P = 450 + 0.5Q_S$

a) Using the equations for demand and supply, what is the equilibrium rent per month and the equilibrium quantity of Aviator Ashleigh's Aviator Lake Cottages traded?

In equilibrium: $Q_D = Q_S = Q^*$

$450 + 0.5Q = 850 - 0.5Q$

$Q^* = 400$ per month

Substitute $Q^* = 400$ in Supply (or, demand)

$P = 450 + 0.5\ (400)$

$P = 450 + 200$

$P^* = \$650$

b) If a rent ceiling of \$500 per month is imposed, what is the quantity of Aviator Ashleigh's Aviator Lake Cottages supplied? What is the quantity of Aviator Ashleigh's Aviator Lake Cottages demanded? Would this create a surplus or a shortage?

$Pc = \$500$

$Q_D = 700$ $Q_S = 100$

Quantity rented $= Q_S$

$Q_D - Q_S = 700 - 100 = 600$ Excess Demand .... Shortage

c) What is the maximum price that a buyer is willing to pay for the last Aviator Ashleigh's Aviator Lake cottage supplied in part (b).

$Q_S = 100$ $[= Q_D = 100]$ in Demand Curve or in schedule

$P = \$800$

Maximum price a buyer is willing to pay for the LAST Aviator Ashleigh's Aviator Lake cottage is \$800.

This is the Black Market price.

From the demand curve: $P = 850 - 0.5\ (100)$

$= 850 - 50$

$P_{MAX} = \$800$

d) If the average wage rate of cottage seekers in Aviator Lake is \$15 per hour, how many hours per month would a potential renter search for a cottage?

$W = \$15/hr$

Premium $= P_{MAX} - Pc = \$800 - \$500 = \$300$

Search $=$ Premium / Wage rate $= \$300\ /\ \$15 = 20$ hours

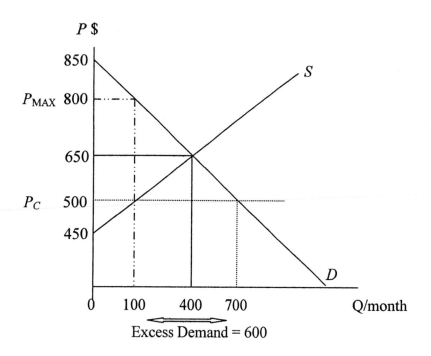

Market for Aviator Ashleigh's Aviator Lake Cottages

e) Suppose now that Aviator Ashleigh (the landlord) were required to pay $100 per Aviator Lake cottage in a renter's tax to the government of Aviator Lake. Show the new supply schedule for cottages. What is the new equilibrium rent and quantity traded of cottages in Aviator Lake? Write down the new equation for supply.

In equilibrium: $Q_D = Q_S = Q^*$	Supply: $P = 450 + 0.5Q_S$
$550 + 0.5Q = 850 - 0.5Q$	Supply decreases by the vertical distance of tax
$Q^* = 300$	$= 100$ [Y-axis intercept increases by amount
substitute in Demand	of tax $(450 + 100 = 550)$]
$P = 850 - 0.5 (300)$	New Supply: $P = 550 + 0.5Q_S$
$P = 850 - 150$	
$P^* = \$700$ [Price or rent paid by the buyer]	

58

f) What is the incidence of the tax (i.e., who actually bears the burden of the tax?)?
   Original price: $P_o = \$650$
   New price is the buyer's price: $P_B = \$700$
   Buyers pay: $\$700 - \$650 = \$50$ tax per unit
   Total burden to the buyer = $\$50 \, (300) = \$15,000$

   Sellers (landlords) remit the entire tax of $100
   Seller's Price: $\$700 - \$100 = \$600$ $P_S = \$600$
   Seller's burden: $\$100 - \$50 = \$50$ tax per unit
     Or, $P_0 - P_S = \$650 - \$600 = \$50$ tax per unit
   Total burden to the seller = $\$50 \, (300) = \$15,000$
   Given the elasticity of the supply and demand curves in this question only, buyers and sellers
   share the burden of the tax equally.

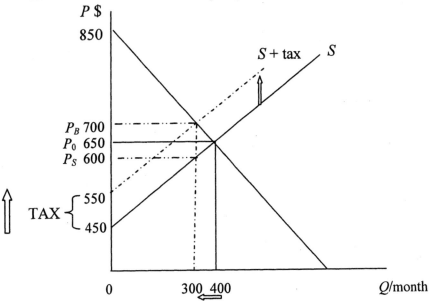

Market for Aviator Ashleigh's Aviator Lake Cottages
Tax to be remitted by sellers

g) Suppose instead that it is the renters (or buyers) rather than the landlords (or sellers) who are
   required to pay the $100 tax to the government of Aviator Lake. Show the new demand
   schedule for cottages. What is the new equilibrium rent and quantity traded of cottages in
   Aviator Lake? Write down the new equation for demand. Who actually bears the burden of
   the tax now?

   In equilibrium: $Q_D = Q_S = Q^*$
   $450 + 0.5Q = 750 - 0.5Q$
   $\qquad Q^* = 300$
   Substitute in supply
   $P = 450 + 0.5 \, (300)$
   $P = 450 + 150$
   $P^* = \$600$ [Price received by seller or landlord]

   Demand: $P = 850 - 0.5Q_D$
   Demand decreases by the vertical distance of tax
   $= 100$ [Y-axis intercept decreases by the amount
   of the tax $(850 - 100 = 750)$]
   New Demand: $P = 750 - 0.5Q_D$

h) How much tax revenue does the government of Aviator Lake collect?
    Buyers remit $600 to landlord + $100 tax to Aviator Lake government = $700 per unit
    Buyer's burden = $700 – $650 = $50 per unit
    Total = $50 (300) = $15,000

    Seller's burden = $650 – $600 = $50 tax per unit
      Or, $100 – $50 = $50 tax per unit
    Total = $50 (300) = $15,000

    Tax revenue = taxes x new equilibrium quantity
                = $100 (300)
                = $30,000
NB: All numbers are the same, regardless of who is to remit the tax.

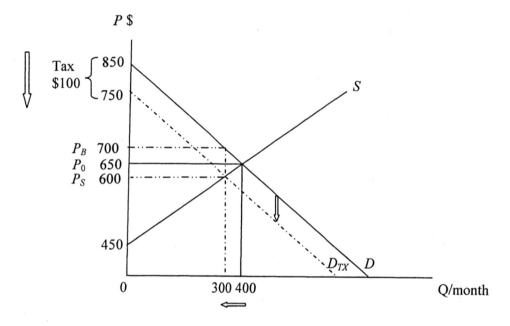

Market for Aviator Ashleigh's Aviator Lake Cottages
Tax to be remitted by the buyers

2. The demand for and the supply of grape pickers (labour) in Aviator Lake are as follows:

Wage Rate (dollars per hour)	Hours Demanded	Hours Supplied	New Hours Demanded
4	3,000	1,000	3,500
5	2,500	1,500	3,000
6	2,000	2,000	2,500
7	1,500	2,500	2,000
8	1,000	3,000	1,500

60

a) What is the equilibrium wage rate in Aviator Lake?

$W^* = \$6/hr$

b) What is the level of employment at the equilibrium wage rate in Aviator Lake?

2000 $\qquad Q_{DL} = Q_{SL} = Q_L^*$

c) What is the level of unemployment at the equilibrium wage rate in Aviator Lake?

Zero unemployment

d) If the government of Aviator Lake imposes a minimum wage of $5 an hour for grape pickers, how many hours do grape pickers work in Aviator Lake?

At $5, minimum wage is below equilibrium—ineffective

$Q_{DL} > Q_{SL} = 2,500 - 1,500 = 1,000$

[Excess demand of labour]

The labour market will move toward equilibrium

Quantity of labour hours = 2,000

Wage rate = $6

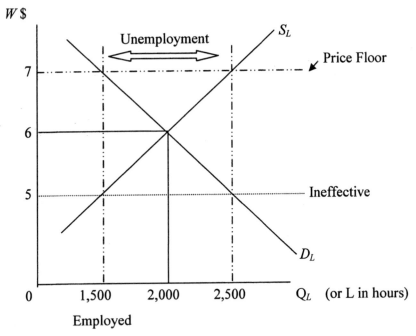

Labour Market for Grape Pickers in Aviator Lake

e) If the government of Aviator Lake imposes a minimum wage of $7 an hour for grape pickers, what are the employment and unemployment levels in Aviator Lake?

Minimum wage is above equilibrium—effective

Employed = $Q_{DL} = 1,500$

Unemployed = $Q_{SL} > Q_{DL} = 2,500 - 1,500 = 1,000$ hours

[Excess supply of labour]

f) If there is a minimum wage of $7 an hour in Aviator Lake and demand increases by 500 hours, what is the level of unemployment in Aviator Lake?

$$At\ \$7\ /hr:\ Q_{DL}' = 1,500 + 500 = 2,000$$
$$Unemployed = Q_{SL}' > Q_{DL}' = 2,500 - 2,000 = 500\ hours$$
[Excess supply of labour]

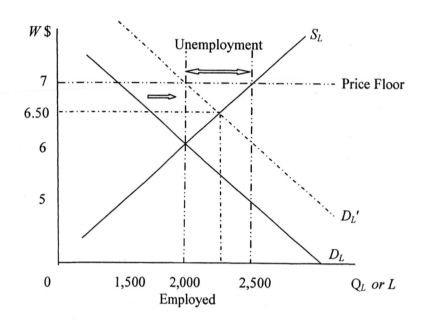

Labour Market for Grape Pickers in Aviator Lake

Minimum Wage = $7
Demand for labour increases by 500 hours to 2,000 hours

Tutorial #5
Chapter 10: *Output and Costs*

Assignment #5: Production Function and Costs

Multiple-Choice Questions:
1. When a firm in Aviator Lake operates its plant at capacity or at its efficient point, it is [c]
a) maximizing profits.
b) producing at its physical limits.
c) producing at the level of output at which marginal cost equals average total cost.
d) producing on the upward-sloping part of its long-run average cost curve.

2. When does a firm in Aviator Lake operate its plant at capacity or at its efficient point? [c]
a) If it is maximizing profits
b) If it is producing at its physical limit
c) If it is producing at the level of output at which marginal cost equals average total cost
d) If it is producing on the upward-sloping part of its long-run average cost curve
Note: Question 1 is stated in sentence-completion format, whereas question 2 is the same multiple-choice question, but given in question format.

3. Suppose Aviator Danilo could triple his production of lumber by tripling his production facility for processing logs. This is an example of [a]
a) constant returns to scale.
b) increasing returns to scale.
c) decreasing returns to scale.
d) the law of diminishing returns.

4. What is an example of Aviator Danilo tripling his production of lumber by tripling his production facility for processing logs? [a]
a) Constant returns to scale
b) Increasing returns to scale
c) Decreasing returns to scale
d) The law of diminishing returns
Note: Question 3 is stated in sentence-completion format, whereas question 4 is the same multiple-choice question, but given in question format.

5. The long-run average cost curve for a firm shows [b]
a) the trend in the average cost of a firm over time
b) the lowest possible average total cost for each level of output when the quantity of all inputs can be changed
c) the lowest possible average total cost for each level of output when the quantity of some but not all inputs can be changed
d) the most likely average total cost for each level of output when the quantity of all inputs are changed

6. What is shown by the long-run average cost curve for a firm? [b]
a) the trend in the average cost of a firm over time.
b) the lowest possible average total cost for each level of output when the quantity of all inputs can be changed.
c) the lowest possible average total cost for each level of output when the quantity of some but not all inputs can be changed.
d) the most likely average total cost for each level of output when the quantity of all inputs are changed.

Note: Question 5 is stated in sentence-completion format, whereas question 6 is the same multiple-choice question, but given in question format.

Short-Answer Questions:
1. Define diminishing marginal returns.
   Diminishing marginal returns occur when more of a variable input can be added to at least one unit of a fixed input and the marginal product of the variable input gradually diminishes.

Problems:
1. The following table shows the monthly output of Aviator Ian's SuperCart Golf Carts (a firm producing very high-powered golf carts) attainable for varying amounts of labour for a given scale of plant as produced by Aviator Ian in Aviator Lake.

Monthly Production of Golf Carts

Labour Workers/mo.	Output Units/mo.	Marginal Product	Average Product
0	0		—
		1	
1	1		1
		2	
2	3		1.5
		3	
3	6		2
		6	
4	12		3
		5	
5	17		3.4
		3	
6	20		3.33
		2	
7	22		3.14
		1	
8	23		2.88

a) Complete the marginal product and average product columns for Aviator Ian's SuperCart Golf Carts in Aviator Lake. Note that the marginal product figures should be entered midway between successive output figures.

64

b) Over what range of workers are marginal returns increasing? With the addition of which worker do diminishing marginal returns begin? Define diminishing marginal returns.
Increasing returns: $L = 0$ to $L = 4$
Diminishing Marginal Returns: with the addition of $L = 5$ (or, after $L = 4$)
When more of a variable input is added to at least 1 unit of a fixed input, the marginal product of the variable input gradually diminishes.

c) At what level of output does Aviator Ian's marginal product equal the average product? How is the value of the marginal product related to the value of the average product? (If you cannot see this by viewing the data, graph the two curves.)
$Q = 17$ $MP = AP = 3.4$

2. Let us examine the short-run costs of Aviator Ian's SuperCart Golf Carts production in Aviator Lake. The information given in the first two columns of the table in problem 1 is repeated in the first two columns of the following table. Assume that the cost of 1 unit of labour (the only variable input) is $2000 per month, and the total fixed cost is $2000 per month.

Short-Run Costs of Aviator Ian's SuperCart Golf Cart production (Monthly, $)

Labour	Output	TFC	TVC	TC	MC	AFC	AVC	ATC
0	0	2000	—	2000		—	—	—
					 2000			
1	1	2000	2000	4000		2000	2000	4000
					 1000			
2	3	2000	4000	6000		666.67	1333.33	2000
					.....666.67			
3	6	2000	6000	8000		333.33	1000	1333.33
					.....333.33			
4	12	2000	8000	10000		166.67	666.67	833.33
					 400			
5	17	2000	10000	12000		117.65	588.24	705.88
					.....666.67			
6	20	2000	12000	14000		100	600	700
					1000			
7	22	2000	14000	16000		90.9	636.36	727.27
					2000			
8	23	2000	16000	18000		86.96	695.65	782.61

a) Complete the table by calculating total fixed cost (TFC), total variable cost (TVC), total cost (TC), marginal cost (MC) (enter midway between successive output levels), average fixed cost (AFC), average variable cost (AVC), and average total cost (ATC) or (AC). Think about the U-shape of the MC, AVC, and ATC curves.

b) At what level of output does the marginal cost cut the average variable cost curve? What is the relationship between the value of the marginal cost and the value of the average variable cost?

Shutdown Point: $P_{min} = \min AVC = MC = 588.24$

Where $P = 588.24$

$Q = 17$

The firm is indifferent at this point.

At any price below this level, the firm would shut down.

At any price above this level, the firm would operate.

c) At what level of output does diminishing marginal returns set in for Aviator Ian's firm, SuperCart Golf Carts? Does this correspond with your answer to problem 1, part (b)?

[Diminishing Marginal Returns: After MP is at a maximum

Or, after MC is at a minimum

MC is at a minimum between $L = 3$ to $L = 4$ (where $Q = 6$ to $Q = 12$) (MC 333.33)]

With the addition of $L = 5$ where $Q = 17$

Or, after $Q = 12$ (after $L = 4$)

Yes, the two answers correspond.

Read the question again. Is the question asking for units of labour or units of output?

d) At what level of output does this firm reach its efficient point? Why? Is the firm at capacity? Is this sometimes called the break-even point? Explain.

Point of efficiency or, capacity or, break-even: where $P = \min ATC = MC$

$P = 700$

$Q = 20$

e) Are economic profits present?

$TC = AC \times q = 700\ (20) = 14{,}000$

$TR = P \times q = 700\ (20) = 14{,}000$

Economic Profits $= TR - TC = 14{,}000 - 14{,}000 = 0$ [Normal Profits]

Or, Economic Profits $= (P - AC)q$

$= (20 - 20)700$

$= 0$

There are zero economic profits or normal profits.

f) What did you notice about the shape of the AVC, ATC, and MC curves?

All these curves are U-shaped. They decrease, reach a minimum, and then begin to increase.

Tutorial #6

Chapter 11: *Perfect Competition*

Assignment #6: Competition: Price Takers

<u>Multiple-Choice Questions:</u>
1. Which of the following is *not* a characteristic of a perfectly competitive industry?   [d]
a) A downward-sloping industry demand curve
b) A perfectly elastic demand curve for each individual firm
c) Each firm decides its quantity of output
d) Each form has slightly differentiated products
e) Many firms each supplying a small fraction of industry supply

2. The characteristic that is **not** present in perfect competition is   [d]
a) a downward-sloping industry demand curve.
b) a perfectly elastic demand curve for each individual firm.
c) each firm decides its quantity of output.
d) each firm has slightly differentiated products.
e) many firms with each supplying a small fraction of industry supply.
<u>Note</u>: Question 1 is stated in question format, whereas question 2 is the same multiple-choice question, but given in sentence-completion format.

3. If economic profits are being made by firms in a competitive industry, new firms will enter. In the short run this will shift   [d]
a) the industry demand curve leftward, causing market price to fall.
b) the industry demand curve rightward, causing market price to rise.
c) the industry supply curve leftward, causing market price to rise.
d) the industry supply curve rightward, causing market price to fall.
e) none of above curves.

4. If economic profits are being made by firms in a competitive industry and new firms enter, what curve will shift in the short run?   [d]
a) The industry demand curve leftward, causing market price to fall
b) The industry demand curve rightward, causing market price to rise
c) The industry supply curve leftward, causing market price to rise
d) The industry supply curve rightward, causing market price to fall
e) None of above curves
<u>Note</u>: Question 3 is stated in sentence-completion format, whereas question 4 is the same multiple-choice question, but given in question format.

5. In a perfectly competitive industry, the market price is $10. An individual firm is producing the output at which $MC = ATC = \$15$. AVC at that output is $10. What should the firm do to maximize its short-run profits? [c]
a) Shut down
b) Expand output
c) Contract output
d) Leave output unchanged
e) Insufficient information to answer

6. When economic profits are zero, [e]
a) the product will not be produced in the short run.
b) the product will not be produced in the long run.
c) firms will leave the industry.
d) revenues are not covering imputed costs.
e) firms are making normal profits.

7. What occurs when economic profits are zero? [e]
a) The product will not be produced in the short run.
b) The product will not be produced in the long run.
c) Firms will leave the industry.
d) Revenues are not covering imputed costs.
e) Firms are making normal profits.
Note: Question 6 is stated in sentence-completion format, whereas question 7 is the same multiple-choice question, but given in question format.

8. The long-run competitive industry supply curve will be positively sloped if there are [b]
a) external economies.
b) external diseconomies.
c) no external economies or diseconomies.
d) external costs.
e) external benefits.

9. When will the long-run competitive industry supply curve will be positively sloped? [b]
a) If there are external economies
b) If there are external diseconomies
c) If there are no external economies or diseconomies
d) If there are external costs
e) If there are external benefits
Note: Question 8 is stated in sentence-completion format, whereas question 9 is the same multiple-choice question, but given in question format.

Short-Answer Questions:

1. The total cost curve for Aaron's Clear Ice Rinks production in Aviator Lake is given as:

$$TC = 3,000 + 60Q + 10Q^2$$

a) Find the total fixed costs and the average fixed costs.

$$TFC = 3,000 \qquad AFC = 3,000 / Q$$

b) Find the total variable costs and the average variable costs.

$$TVC = 60Q + 10Q^2 \qquad AVC = 60 + 10Q$$

c) Find the average total costs.

$$ATC = \frac{3,000}{Q} + 60 + 10Q$$

Problems:

1. The following data are for a firm, R&M Brewery that sells its output, premium beer, in a perfectly competitive market. There are 4 firms in this industry. Assume that the minimum point of the short-run average total cost curve (ATC) is coincident with the minimum point of the long-run average cost curve (LRAC).

Quantity Output	Total Cost	Total Variable Cost	Marginal Cost	Average Cost	Average Variable Cost
0	50	—		—	—
			40		
1	90	40		90	40
			30		
2	120	70		60	35
			20		
3	140	90		46.67	30
			30		
4	170	120		42.50	30
			40		
5	210	160		42	32
			50		
6	260	210		43.33	35
			60		
7	320	270		45.71	38.57
			80		
8	400	350		50	43.75

NB: Marginal costs are set between the lines.

a) If the market price for this product is $55 per unit, what is the profit-maximizing output of each firm? Explain. What is the industry output?

$P = MC$ $P = MC = \$55$ $q = 6$

Number of firms = 4

Number of firms x $q = Q$

$$4\,(6) = 24$$
$$Q = 24$$

b) What is the economic profit/loss of each firm?

Economic Profit $= [P - AC]\,q$

$$= \ [55 - 43.33]\,6$$
$$= \ 11.67\,(6)$$
$$= \ \$70.02$$

c) At approximately what output level would this firm, R&M Brewery, be efficient in the short run?

$P = MC = \min ATC = \$42$ $q = 5$

Total Revenue = Total Costs   Normal Profits   Zero Economic Profits

Point of Efficiency of the Firm or Capacity of the Firm

d) If the market price for the product, premium beer was $29, how much output would this firm, R&M Brewery, produce?

$P < \min AVC = \$29$ $q = 0$

e) At what output level would this firm shut down in the short run? Explain your answer.

$P = \min AVC = MC = \$30$ is the Shutdown point $q = 4$

When $P < \min AVC$, the firm will shut down

f) Draw a simple graph for the firm, R&M Brewery, showing the market price, profit-maximizing output, break-even point, and shutdown point. Label all curves accurately.

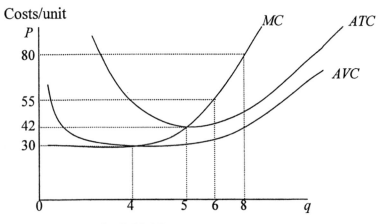

Cost Curves for R&M Brewery

70

g) Construct R&M Brewery's short-run supply curve of output.

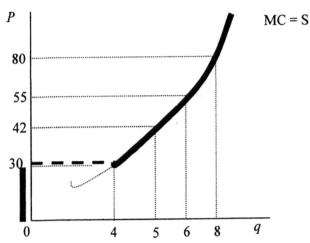

R&M Brewery's Short-Run Supply Curve

$P = MC = \$30 \quad q = 4$
$P = MC = \$42 \quad q = 5$
$P = MC = \$55 \quad q = 6$
$P = MC = \$80 \quad q = 8$
- Begin at origin and follow the y-axis to the price minimum
- The shutdown point $P = 30$ and $q = 4$ must be included
- One or two other points are of your choosing

h) State the condition for long-run equilibrium of a firm. At what price and output would this firm, R&M Brewery, be in long-run equilibrium?

$P_{LR} = \min LRAC = MC_{LR}$
$\quad\quad = \min SRAC = MC_{SR}$
$P = \$42 \quad q = 5$
$TR = TC$
Normal profits

71

Tutorial #7

Chapter 12: *Monopoly*

Assignment #7: Market Power: Single-Price Monopoly

Multiple-Choice Questions:
1. Suppose a monopolist can sell 33 units of output per day for a price of $12 each and 34 units of output per day for $11.75 each. The marginal revenue for the 34th unit sold is equal to [b]
a) $0.
b) $3.50.
c) $11.75.
d) 25 cents.
e) uncertain, as not enough information is given to compute the marginal revenue.

2. Four monopolists were overheard talking at the LP Café. Which one of their statements that follow contains a correct strategy for maximizing profits?   [d]
a) "We only increase output when we know that a greater output will raise total revenue".
b) "Cost minimization is the best way to maximizing profits".
c) "We try to make the most of our equipment by producing at maximum capacity".
d) "I don't continually look at total profits, but I do try to make sure that any new business deals increase my revenues more than they increase my costs".
e) None of the above.

3. A natural monopoly is defined as an industry in which   [a]
a) one firm is able to produce the entire industry output at a lower average cost than other group of firms could.
b) one firm is able to produce the entire industry output at a lower marginal cost than any other group of firms could.
c) one firm is very large relative to other firms entering the industry.
d) a singular firm is able to earn higher profits in an industry than if additional firms enter the same industry.

Short-Answer Questions:
1. Suppose that in the short run, every perfectly competitive firm within an industry was earning economic profits. Use diagrams to show the following:
a) What happens to the industry supply curve and, hence, the perfectly competitive market price?
▪ More firms enter the industry.
▪ Industry supply curve increases, shifts rightward.
▪ Prices decrease.
▪ Industry output increases.
▪ Firms enter until economic profits are zero or normal profits exist.

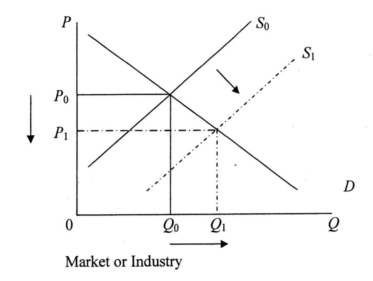

Market or Industry

b) What happens to the demand curve facing each and every individual firm?
 ▪ Firms are price takers.
 ▪ Firms take the lower industry price.
 ▪ This designates their lower demand curve, D_1.
 ▪ $P = MC$.
 ▪ Output for the individual firm decreases.
 ▪ Firms reach their point of efficiency where $P = MC = $ min. ATC.

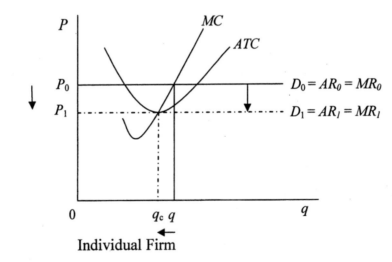

Individual Firm

c) If the short- and long-run average total cost curves are coincident at their minimum points, at what price and output level will each firm (and, hence, the industry as a whole) be in long-run equilibrium? [Hint: It will help you here to state the long-run equilibrium condition.]

$P_{LR} = $ min. $LRAC$
    $= MC_{LR}$
    $= $ min. $SRAC$
    $= MC_{SR}$

Output is at capacity $= q_c$ *Or*, output is at it's point of efficiency $= q_{eff}$.

73

Firm is operating at its point of efficiency.

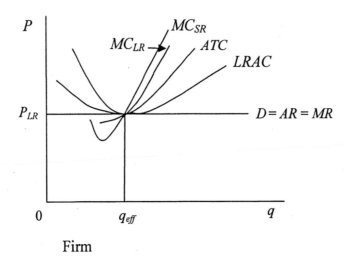

Firm

Problems:
1. The following diagram shows the cost and revenue information for a monopolist. Aviator Rylan's Fine Wines is the only vineyard and winery on the Island of Aviator Lake.

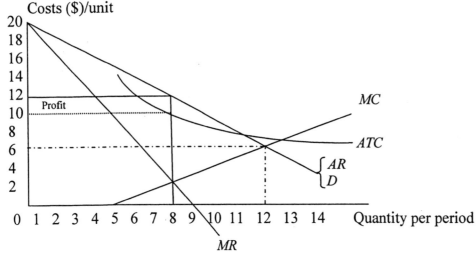

Aviator Rylan's Fine Wines of Aviator Lake

a) For Aviator Rylan's Fine Wines, a profit-maximizing monopolist, what is the monopoly price? What is the monopoly output?

$MR = MC$ $P = 12$ $q = 8$ $[TR = 12 (8) = 96]$

b) What is the monopoly profit for Aviator Rylan's Fine Wines?

$P = 12$ $q = 8$ $ATC = 10$
Economic Profit $= [12 - 10]$ 8
$\qquad = 2 (8)$
$\qquad = \$16$

c) At what output would the monopolist, Aviator Rylan's Fine Wines, maximize revenue?

At $q = 9$ where $MR = 0$ $TR =$ Maximum $[TR = 9 (11) = 99]$

d) Suppose that this market for Aviator Rylan's Fine Wines was organized as a perfectly competitive industry, instead of a monopoly. What would be the perfectly competitive price and industry output? How does it compare to the monopoly price and output?

$P = MC = \$6$ $q = 12$

Price is lower.   Quantity is greater   Society's welfare is maximized.

2. The Pointed Needle Co., run by Melissa and Michal, has the monopoly for making aviator jackets.

Its demand curve is: $P = 30 - 0.2Q$

where Q is quantity demanded and P is price per aviator jacket in dollars.

Its marginal cost curve is: $MC = 6 + 0.6Q$

where Q is quantity produced per day and MC is marginal cost per aviator jackets in dollars.

Its marginal revenue curve is: $MR = 30 - 0.4Q$

where Q is quantity sold and MR is marginal revenue per aviator jacket in dollars.

a) Calculate the profit-maximizing price and quantity of aviator jackets for this monopoly, the Pointed Needle that is run by Melissa and Michal.

Set profit-maximization: $MR = MC$

$6 + 0.6\,Q = 30 - 0.4\,Q$

$0.6\,Q + 0.4\,Q = 30 - 6$

$\qquad Q = 24$ aviator jackets per day

Substitute $Q = 24$ in to the demand curve

$P = 30 - 0.2\,Q$

$P = 30 - 0.2\,(24)$

$P = 30 - 4.8$

$P = \$25.20$

b) If, instead, the market for aviator jackets was organized as a perfectly competitive industry, what price would be charged for aviator jackets? How many aviator jackets will be produced?

Set profit-maximization: $P = MC$ At the Demand Curve

$6 + 0.6\,Q = 30 - 0.2\,Q$

$0.6\,Q + 0.2\,Q = 30 - 6$

$\qquad 0.8\,Q = 24$

$\qquad Q = 24 / 0.8$

$\qquad Q = 30$ aviator jackets per day

Substitute $Q = 30$ in Demand

$P = 30 - 0.2\,Q$

$P = 30 - 0.2\,(30)$

$P = 30 - 6$

$P = \$24$

c) Which market structure gives a lower price and a larger output for aviator jackets?

<u>Perfectly Competitive Market</u> is efficient

- One of many firms
- Price taker—no control over price
   - No incentive to manipulate the market by altering price and output
- No barriers to entry
- Many buyers

- Identical product—close substitutes
  Monopoly is inefficient
- One firm
- No close substitutes, unique product
- Barriers to entry
- Considerable control over price
- Profit-maximizes where $MR = MC$
  - Restricts output
  - Charges a higher price
  - Demand curve is a constraint and therefore $P > MC$

d) Calculate the consumers' surplus when the industry is assumed to be perfectly competitive.

$P = 30 - 0.2\,Q$
when $Q = 0$
$P = 30$ (y-axis intercept)

$P = MC$ at Demand

CS = Area $\triangle\,ABC$
$= \frac{1}{2}$ base x height
$= \frac{1}{2}\,[30\,(30 - 24)]$
$= \frac{1}{2}\,[30\,(6)]$
$= \frac{1}{2}\,(180)$
$= \$90$

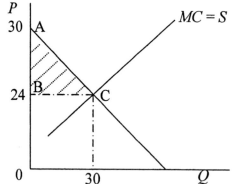

e) Calculate the consumers' surplus portion of the deadweight loss when the industry is assumed to be a monopoly.

DWL in Consumer Surplus = Area $\triangle\,DEC$
$= \frac{1}{2}\,[b \text{ x } h]$
$= \frac{1}{2}\,[(30 - 24)\,(25.20 - 24)]$
$= \frac{1}{2}\,[6\,(1.20)]$
$= \frac{1}{2}\,[7.2]$
$= \$3.60$

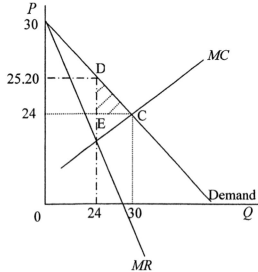

76

3. On the following diagram of a natural monopoly, Rob and Pete's Excellent Mountain Adventures: (1) show marginal cost pricing and label the price P_{eff} and the quantity Q_{eff}, and (2) show average cost pricing and label the price P_{ac} and the quantity Q_{ac}.

(1) Marginal Cost Pricing

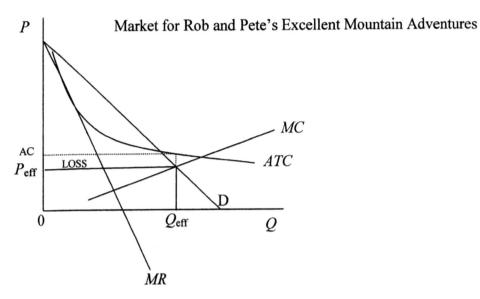

- Marginal cost pricing is a regulated price set by the government of Aviator Lake.
- Rob and Pete would incur a loss.
- Rob and Pete would not continue to operate if they were required to incur this loss.
- The government of Aviator Lake (the taxpayers) would have to subsidize this monopoly an amount equal to the loss.

(2) Average Cost Pricing

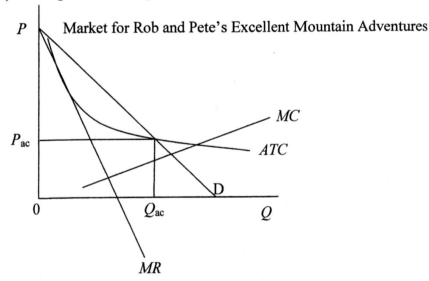

- Price equals average costs.
- Rob and Pete are earning normal profits or zero economic profits.

Tutorial #8

Chapter 17: *Demand and Supply in Factor Markets*

Assignment #8: Labour Market

Multiple-Choice Questions:
1. The marginal revenue product of labour in Aviator Lake is   [c]
a) the extra income a worker receives by working an extra hour.
b) the extra profit a firm earns by employing an additional worker.
c) the extra total revenue resulting from hiring one additional worker.
d) the extra output resulting from hiring an additional worker.

2. Which of the following statements is *not* true about the demand for a factor of production in Aviator Lake?   [b]
a) It is more elastic, the more elastic the demand for the final product
b) It is more elastic in cases where technology does not permit substitution with other factors
c) It is less elastic the smaller its contribution to the total cost of the product
d) It is more elastic the longer the time period considered

3. As the wage rate increases, the substitution effect will give a household an incentive to [c]
a) raise its reservation wage
b) increase its nonmarket activity and decrease its market activity
c)   increase its market activity and decrease its nonmarket activity
d) increase both market and nonmarket activities

4. The income effect of a higher wage rate in Aviator Lake refers to   [d]
a) the increase in the workers' purchasing power due to the higher wage rate.
b) the fact that workers have to be paid a higher income if they are to be influenced to work longer hours.
c) the change in the prices of consumer goods that follows an increase in worker's incomes as wage rates increase.
d) the increase in demand for leisure that is generated by an increase in the worker's wage rate (or income).

5. As the wage rate continues to rise in Aviator Lake, a household will have a backward-bending supply of labour curve if   [c]
a) the income effect and the substitution effect are moving in the same direction.
b) the wage rate is higher than the reservation wage.
c) the income effect dominates over the substitution effect.
d) the substitution effect dominates over the income effect.

Short-Answer Questions:
1. Define and draw the marginal revenue product of labour.
   Marginal revenue product of labour is the change in total revenue that results from the use of an extra until of labour. Or, the additional revenue earned from the sale of output generated by hiring one more unit of labour.

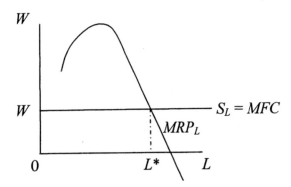

- The shape of the marginal revenue product of labour curve results from the shape of the marginal product of labour
- $MRP_L = MP_L * MR$ where MR is the price of the output
- $MRP_L = \dfrac{\Delta TR}{\Delta L}$

Profit-maximize by hiring labour until $W = MRP_L$

2. Define transfer earnings. Define economics rent.
   Transfer Earnings: The income required to induce the supply of a factor—opportunity cost.
   Economic Rent: The income received by the owner of the factor over and above the transfer earnings.

Problems:
1. You are given the following information about the labour market at the northeastern portion of Aviator Lake. Everyone in this area works for logging companies, but there are many logging companies in the area. The market for logging workers is perfectly competitive, and the demand and supply curves for logging workers are as follows:
   Demand: $Q_{DL} = 480 - 40W$
   Supply: $Q_{SL} = 40 + 40W$
   where Q_{SL} = quantity supplied of labour in hours
   Q_{DL} = quantity demanded of labour in hours
   W = wage rate/hour

a) What is the equilibrium wage rate and quantity of hours employed in the logging industry in Aviator Lake?
   In equilibrium: $Q_{DL} = Q_{SL} = Q_L{}^*$
   $40 + 40W = 480 - 40W$
       $80W = 440$
         $W = 440 / 80$
      $W* = \$5.50$ per hour
   Substitute $W = \$360$ in Supply
     $Q_L = 40 + [40 (5.50)]$
     $Q_L = 40 + 220$
     $Q_L{}^* = 260$ hours   [or, L = 260 hours]

b) What is the total labour income in logging in Aviator Lake?
Total labour income = W x Q_L
$$= 5.50\ (260)$$
$$= \$1430$$

c) How much of the labour income in Aviator Lake as found in part (b) is economic rent and how much is transfer earnings?

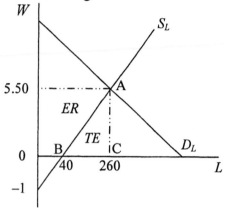

Labour Market for Logging in Aviator Lake

TE = ½ bh of $\triangle ABC$ $Q_{SL} = 40 + 40W$
    = ½ [(260 – 40) (5.5)]   When $W = 0$
    = ½ [(220) (5.5)] $Q_{SL} = 40$
    = ½ (1210) X-axis intercept
TE = $605
Total Income – Transfer Earnings = Economic Rent
$1430 – 605 = \$825
Economic Rent = $825

2. M&M Surf is a small firm making contoured boogie boards in Brian's Bay in Aviator Lake. The firm sells its product in a competitive market and buys labour in a competitive market. M&M Surf sells its contoured boogie boards for $150 each, and it has no trouble finding workers willing to work for the market wage of $300 per week.

a) Complete the MRP_L column in the following table by calculating the marginal revenue product of labour for M&M Surf.

b) The values obtained for MRP_L will be the same if they are calculated by using either of the following formulas:

$MRP_L = MP$ x MR or,

$MRP_L = \dfrac{\Delta TR}{\Delta L}$

where MR = marginal revenue of a unit of output
      MP = marginal product of the factor
      ΔTR = change in total revenue from the output
      ΔL = change in the quantity of labour employed

80

Show that this is the case when the quantity of labour employed (Petra and Adam) is 2 workers per week.

$L = 2$ $MRP_L = MP \times MR$

$\qquad\qquad\qquad\qquad = 5\,(150)$

$\qquad\qquad\qquad\qquad = 750$

At $L = 1$ $TR = 6\,(150)$ $MRP_L = \Delta TR / \Delta L$

$\qquad\qquad = 900$ $= [750 / 1]$

At $L = 2$ $TR = 11\,(150)$ $= 750$

$\qquad\qquad = 1650$

$\Delta TR = 1650 - 900 = 750$

Total Output and Marginal Revenue Product of Labour at M&M Surf

Quantity Labour Hired/Week	Total Output /Week	MP_L	MR	MRP_L $ /Week
0	0	—		
1	6	6	150	900
2	11	5	150	750
3	15	4	150	600
4	18	3	150	450
5	20	2	150	300
6	21	1	150	150

Assume: M&M Surf is a profit-maximizing firm.

Price of Output (contoured boogie boards) = $MR = \$150$

NB: For ease, the MP_L was dropped onto the next line rather than stated between the lines.

c) How many workers will M&M Surf employ if the price of contoured boogie boards is $150 each and the market wage is $300 per week? How many contoured boogie boards will the firm produce?

Set Profit Maximization: $W = MRP_L = \$300$ $\left(\begin{array}{c} W = MRP_L \\ MFC = MRP_L \\ MC_L = MRP_L \end{array} \right)$

$L = 5$ $Q = 20$

d) Show that at this profit-maximizing level of output, marginal revenue is equal to marginal cost. [Recall that marginal cost can be calculated as the price of the variable factor (labour) divided by the marginal product of the variable factor.]

Profit Maximize where $P_Q = MR = MC$ at $Q = 20$

$MC = \dfrac{\Delta TVC}{\Delta Q} = \dfrac{W}{MP_L} = \dfrac{300}{2} = \$150$

Therefore, $MC = MR = P_Q$ where $W = MRP_L$

e) If total fixed cost is $1,000 per week, how much is M&M Surf's profit per week?

At $Q = 20$: $TFC = \$1,000$

$\qquad\qquad TVC = W \times L = 300\,(5) = \$1,500$

$\qquad\qquad TC = TFC + TVC = 1,000 + 1,500 = \$2,500$

$\qquad\qquad TR = P \times Q = 150\,(20) = \$3,000$

Economic Profit = $TR - TC = 3,000 - 2,500 = \$500$ per week

f) What will M&M Surf's profit be if the firm employs one more worker each week?

$\Delta L = +1$ At $L = 6$

$TR = 150\,(21)$

    $= \$3150$

$TC = 1{,}000 + [6\,(300)]$

    $= 1{,}000 + 1{,}800$

    $= \$2{,}800$

Economic Profit $= 3{,}150 - 2{,}800 = \$350$

NB: At $L = 5$ profit of \$500 is greater than profit of \$350 at $L = 6$

g) Draw a graph of M&M Surf's demand for labour, showing the supply of labour facing the firm and indicate the quantity of labour employed by the firm.

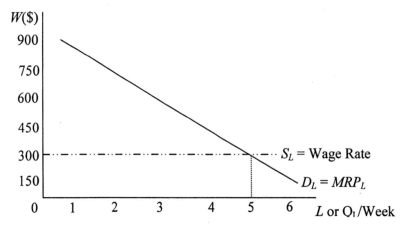

Market for Labour for M&M Surf

Tutorial #9

Chapter 2/32: *Trading with the World*

Assignment #9: Gains from Trade

Multiple-Choice Questions:
1. In an eight-hour day, Melissa can produce either 24 dozen muffins or 8 cases of jam. In an eight-hour day, Michal can produce either 8 dozen muffins or 8 cases of jam.   [c]
a) Melissa has the lower opportunity cost of producing muffins, whereas Melissa and Michal have equal opportunity costs of producing jam.
b) Melissa has the higher opportunity cost of producing both muffins and jam.
c) Melissa has the lower opportunity cost of producing muffins, whereas Michal has the lower opportunity cost of producing jam.
d) Melissa has the lower opportunity cost of producing jam, whereas Michal has the lower opportunity cost of producing muffins.

2. Ashleigh and Adam can produce the following in one week: [a]

Ashleigh		Adam	
Rooms	Cars	Rooms	Cars
8	0	20	0
6	1	15	2
4	2	10	4
2	3	5	6
0	4	0	8

where Rooms is the number of rooms designed and Cars is the number of cars repaired. Given this information, can Ashleigh and Adam gain by specialization?
a) Yes, unconditionally
b) No, not under the given circumstances
c) It depends on the wages each earns
d) Only if they are married to each other

3. It pays people to specialize and trade with each other because   [d]
a) otherwise they could not survive.
b) they can take advantage of the fact they have an absolute advantage in the production of something.
c) otherwise they cannot sell the food for which they have a higher opportunity cost.
d) they can consume outside their production possibilities frontier.

Short-Answer Questions:
1. Define comparative advantage.
   Comparative advantage: When a person or country is able to produce a good at the lowest opportunity cost.

2. Define absolute advantage.
   Absolute advantage: When a person or country is able to produce more of all goods than someone else or has a higher rate of productivity in the production of all goods.

Problems:
1. Suppose that two islands, Aviator Lake and Terryland, have the output figures shown in the following table. Two goods are produced: boogie boards and golf clubs.

Average Product per Worker

Country	Boogie Boards	or	Golf Clubs
Aviator Lake	8		4
Terryland	8		6

a) What is the opportunity cost of producing a boogie board in Aviator Lake?
   1 more boogie board opportunity cost = 4/8 =1/2 or 0.5 golf clubs
b) What is the opportunity cost of producing a golf club in Aviator Lake?
   1 more golf club opportunity cost = 8/4 = 2 boogie boards
c) What is the opportunity cost of producing a boogie board in Terryland?
   1 more boogie board opportunity cost = 6/8 or 0.75 golf clubs
d) What is the opportunity cost of producing a golf club in Terryland?
   1 more golf club opportunity cost = 8/6 or 1.33 boogie boards
e) In what product does the Aviator Lake have a comparative advantage?
   Boogie boards (lower opportunity cost—only gives up 0.5 golf clubs)
f) In what product does Terryland have a comparative advantage?
   Golf clubs (lower opportunity cost—only gives up 1.33 boogie boards)
g) Suppose that the labour force in Aviator Lake is 5 million, and the labour force is 10 million in Terryland.
   Fill in the missing production possibilities data for both countries in the tables.

Aviator Lake's Production Possibilities (million of units)

	A	B	C	D	E
Boogie Boards	40	30	20	10	0
Golf Clubs	0	5	10	15	20

Terryland's Production Possibilities (millions of units)

	A	B	C	D	E
Boogie Boards	80	60	40	20	0
Golf Clubs	0	15	30	45	60

h) Suppose that both countries are presently producing at combination D. Show the joint totals before trade in the following table:

Total Output in Millions of Units

	Boogie Boards	Golf Clubs
Aviator Lake	10	15
Terryland	20	45
Total: Both countries	30	60

i) Now suppose that each country specializes in the product in which it has a comparative advantage. Show the new totals after trade in the following table:

Total Output in Millions of Units

	Boogie Boards	Golf Clubs
Aviator Lake	40	0
Terryland	0	60
Total: Both countries	40	60

j) As a result, the joint gain from trade is equal to:
    __10__ boogie boards,   __0__ golf clubs.

Explanation:

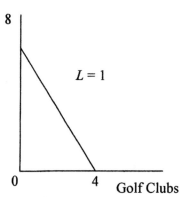

Aviator Lake
Population: 5 million
Comparative Advantage in: Boogie Boards

Terryland
Population: 10 million
Comparative Advantage in: Golf Clubs

AP_L in golf clubs = 4

Point "E": boogie boards = 0

AP_L in boogie boards = 8

Point "A": golf clubs = 0

All golf clubs
Population x AP_L = 5 (4) = 20

All boogie boards
Population x AP_L = 10 (8) = 80

<u>Aviator Lake</u>

1 boogie board opportunity cost = 0.5 golf club

From "E" to "D" = 10 boogie boards
10 boogie boards opportunity cost = 10 (0.5) = 5 golf clubs
Point "D" = 20 − 5 = 15 golf clubs
Point "C" = 15 − 5 = 10 golf clubs
Point "B" = 10 − 5 = 5 golf clubs
Point "A" = 5 − 5 = 0 golf clubs

<u>Terryland</u>

1 golf clubs opportunity cost = 1.33 boogie boards

From "A" to "B" = 15 golf clubs
15 golf clubs opportunity cost = 15 (1.33) = 19.95 ≈ 20 boogie boards

Point "B" = 80 − 20 = 60 boogie boards
Point "C" = 60 − 20 = 40 boogie boards
Point "D" = 40 − 20 = 20 boogie boards
Point "E" = 20 − 20 = 0 boogie boards

With specialization: endpoint solution—each country produces only that good in which it has a comparative advantage. Gains from trade: increase consumption possibilities, but **not** production possibilities.

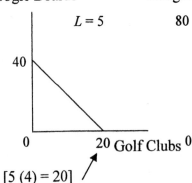

Aviator Lake

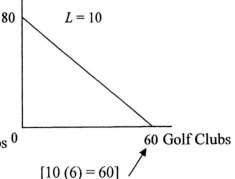

Terryland

86